Diary of a
Girl in Changi
1941–45

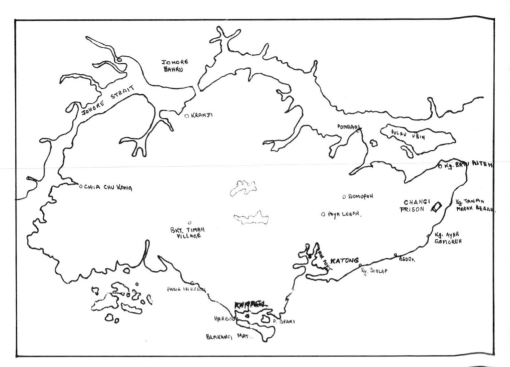

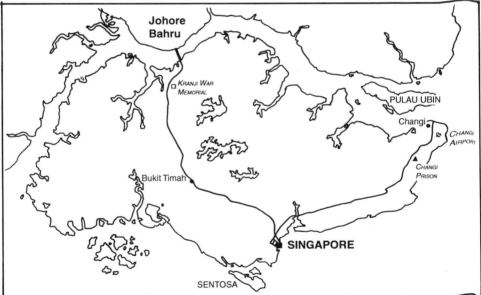

Top: Map of Singapore drawn by the author for a tablecloth pattern she embroidered while in Changi.
Bottom: Singapore today.

Diary of a
GIRL IN CHANGI
1941–45

Sheila Allan

Kangaroo Press

To my father's memory
and to those internees who shared my life
during those three and a half years in Changi
Prison and Sime Road Camp

Acknowledgments

Special thanks to my daughter Sandra for her support and encouragement and to Carl Harrison-Ford whose help and advice meant so much in the writing of this record.

First published in 1994 by Kangaroo Press Pty Ltd
3 Whitehall Road Kenthurst NSW 2156 Australia
P.O. Box 6125 Dural Delivery Centre NSW 2158
Typeset by G.T. Setters Pty Limited
Printed by Star Printery Pty Ltd, Erskineville 2043

ISBN 0 86417 619 8

Contents

Introduction

'Selamat jalan'—little did I realise how much those words would come to mean when uttered by our Chinese cook boy, Ah Juan, as he bade us farewell. Did he guess the road we had to travel needed all the luck available, I wonder?

'A pleasant or safe journey' one says in English, and in French it is *'Bon voyage'*. The same meaning is found in that Malayan phrase—*'Selamat jalan'*.

It seems so long—over fifty years—since the beginning of our journey, and sometimes I find it difficult to believe that I have come this far and have been so lucky to be alive today. This diary is only an account of just one girl—a seventeen-year-old girl who had turned twenty-one by the end of the Pacific War. It is not a war story—it isn't meant to be—only a record of the experiences and reactions of one who went through those hazardous days of 1941-5.

From a collection of exercise books and scraps of paper that have been gathering dust over the years I will try to reassemble my diary. However, the writing on some of them has faded a little and there are some pages missing—so I may have to think back hard, to try to remember some of the events. Together we'll travel the road again from danger to safety as I have done.

I was born in Taiping in 1924. My father, John Charles Allan, was an Australian, from Melbourne, who worked as a mining engineer and dredgemaster for Osborne & Chappel Company. My mother was a Malayan and, as the diary indicates, I know little of her though my memories are sometimes troubled ones. My family went to live in Penang and I started school as a day pupil in Penang Convent. Not much later my father was sent to Siam and was stationed at Paktak.

Some of my happiest memories are of that village where I used to visit my father once a year at Christmas, on holidays from the convent where I was then boarding. I had no children to play with but for company had two dogs, a Siamese cat and a monkey. There was a Chinese amah and a Chinese cook to take care of our meals.

Before my father left for work each morning, he used to set two pages from the dictionary for me to learn the spelling and meaning of each word and then to write sentences using them. I guess I got into the habit of writing things down and I'm still doing it. Certainly I had a desire to be a writer at the time of my internment though my father, perhaps unusually for those days, wanted me to become an engineer.

In 1939 my father returned to Malaya and was stationed at Kampar, about sixteen miles from Ipoh. Transferred from Taiping Convent to Ipoh Convent in 1936, I completed my education in November 1941 and returned to my father, who had married a Siamese woman, Vichim, earlier that year. The three of us went up to the Cameron Highlands for the holidays before I was to leave for Melbourne, where my father wanted me to enter the university, although I had other ideas. However, neither of our plans came to fruition as Japan invaded Malaya early in December, while we were still on holidays. The main events of my life for the almost four years that followed are recorded in the diary I kept.

Although I was seventeen when the war broke out, I was a very, very young seventeen-year-old—idealistic, a dreamer, a romantic and more than a little innocent! I thought the world was full of beautiful people. Indeed, though the brief but brutal Malayan Campaign and the three and a half years of internment that followed exposed me to many of the harsher realities of life, I maintained a belief in human decency and dignity and the behaviour of most of my fellow internees in Changi Prison and, later, Sime Road Camp allowed me to continue to hold that belief.

To some, my diary of day-to-day activities for that period may appear rather mundane, and if readers expect to read about shocking brutality and rapes then they'll be disappointed. Certainly other internees in other camps—and of course the military POWs—suffered harsher treatment, much of it that defies credulity. But the threat of such barbaric treatment was real to all of the women interned, especially the young ones, and we were none of us strangers to hunger, disease, lack of adequate medical supplies, and other pressures that resulted in occasional bouts of despair, some madness, and even a number of suicides. As well, the isolation and cooped-up nature of our existence produced its fair share of tensions between internees and even political intrigue, though my diary deals only fleetingly with the latter.

As for the diary itself, it was a dangerous undertaking, and the consequences of its discovery could have been horrendous. But I had to do something to keep my sanity and, for an aspiring writer, what better option than to record (dangerous an undertaking as it was) how we lived, what we did to keep ourselves from getting bored, and how the camp was run—in as near to a civilised manner as an uncivilised situation would allow.

It was a communal life of sorts, with elected supervisors for each section to see that chores were given to each of us and carried out as instructed. A school for the children was started, somewhat surreptitiously, and the adolescents like myself had the responsibility of looking after the younger internees. As the diary also reveals, there were many concerts and other entertainments, lectures on cultural and other subjects, and even literary competitions that were subject to the most rigorous of assessment. I threw myself into all these activities. There was also a perhaps very British air of formality that helped keep our community together. Formal invitations were issued for 'elevenses' and the like; many camp entertainments had printed programmes; birthday and Christmas cards were exchanged; and the letters of condolence I received from many internees when my father died in June 1945—only weeks before the Japanese surrender—helped me come to terms with my grief.

We were a motley crew of humanity for all that, with different nationalities, ages, religions and levels of education. There were teachers, doctors and nurses who looked after our health to the extent medical supplies were available—which was practically nil at times—but we had our own internees, and not the Japanese, to look after us.

Looking back, we were an enterprising lot. We managed to keep our sense of humour in spite of the ugliness, the discomfort, the hunger, the gloom and doom of our existence. We also knew the true meaning of 'mateship'.

Rereading the diary I commenced writing over fifty years ago brings back vividly both the events described and the circumstances in which I recorded them. No one knew that I kept a diary at the time and, fully aware of the risk that I was taking, I told no one. Everyone thought I was writing stories and verses just to pass the time, which in fact I was also doing. As a safeguard, I hid the diary amongst other papers and books in my quarters, though camp inspections never failed to fill me with dread.

As well, I was often as cryptic as possible in my diary entries. People referred to by a letter only, or a nickname, were described thus in the original entries. In a war there are always fifth-columnists around and all internees had to be extremely careful in conversation, often speaking in riddles. In transcribing the diary I have retained these subterfuges, believing the original tone conveys the circumstances and pressures—from lack of paper through to fear of the diary's discovery—of the time. In retrospect it appears that I was not really cryptic enough in my references to certain events!

Some explanations have been added in square brackets, but I have kept these to a minimum. Occasionally I have added a word or two where silverfish ate the original, and I have sometimes corrected spelling or grammatical errors, though never to an extent that masks the pressures and conditions under which I wrote. Other than that, the diary has only been abridged by the removal of a number of poems, lists of names in accounts of camp concerts, many extracts from camp newsletters and public notices that I took down at the time, and my description of the trip from Singapore to Australia in November 1945. The complete diary has been lodged with the Australian War Memorial, Canberra.

I had no intention of having my diary published when I started writing it, or for more than forty years after I completed it. For the months immediately after the Japanese surrender I still wrote, recording how I fell (hopelessly) in love with the British airman 'Jinx' Gordon. At least I think it was love as it was an emotion I'd never felt before. He left for England in late October 1945 and the following month my father's sister, Grace Allan, with the help of the Australian Red Cross, brought me to Melbourne. My last entry for my internment diary is dated 24 November 1945.

In 1946 I started my training as a nurse at the Queen Victoria Memorial Hospital for Women by Women, graduating in 1949 and working in country hospitals and the Queen Victoria before marrying Frank Bruhn in 1958 and coming to Sydney, where we had a son and a daughter. My husband died in 1986 after a short illness.

I never did talk much about the war and camp life after 1945. My diaries were packed away and did not come to light until two years ago, when my daughter-in-law discovered them under the house. It was suggested then that I should get them in order and make them into a book for the family. But I kept putting it off until the realisation grew that not many people know there were women and children interned in Changi Prison under the Japanese Occupation. When I did mention that I was a Japanese Civilian POW, many people thought I must have been in the armed forces!

When I read that the children's book written by Sir David Griffin when a POW—*The Happiness Box*—was to be published, I went to the launching, hoping there might be some others who were in camp with me. Alas, there was no one else, but I introduced myself to Sir David and it was his wife who suggested that I go back to Singapore for the fiftieth anniversary of the fall of the city in February 1992—a trip that is described in the Postscript to this book. At about the same time I was fortunate in meeting up with fellow internees Elizabeth Ennis—a nurse in the British Indian Army who started the Girl Guide movement in camp—and Mary Scarlett (née Trevor), who was fourteen when she was interned.

For many years I had planned to go back and look for my father's grave and this was an ideal opportunity for me to do so. I located his grave with the help of my friend Mary Lim (née Winters), another ex-internee with whom I had kept in touch over the years, and arrangements are now being made for a headstone. Then, perhaps, this story and this journey will be completed.

But for now I bid you once again *'Selamat jalan'* till we meet again at the end of the trail which began in the Cameron Highlands of Malaya in December 1941.

Sheila Allan
Sydney, January 1994

1941

> The idle life I lead
> Is like a pleasant sleep
> Wherein I rest and heed
> The dreams that by me sweep,
> And still of all my dreams
> In turn so swiftly past,
> Each in its fancy seems
> A nobler than the last;
> And every eve I say,
> Noting my step in bliss,
> I have known no day
> In all my life like this.
>   —Robert Bridges

Alas! How true the last two lines, for today marked the beginning of the 'Malayan War'!

War? Impossible! It can't be! My whole being cried against it for shattering the peace of my holidays up in the hills; for intruding into my calm uneventful life; for making me feel both afraid and excited. In fact, I resented it for causing an emotional upset that was strange to me.

Up in these hills have I been happy, away from the crowds and bustle of town life. Here, have I enjoyed the quiet of the mountain air and stream; here, where one can be free to indulge in one's own thoughts with no outside interference. And what happens? War! Presto—the whole atmosphere is charged with that little three-letter word!

And yet, this morning when I opened my eyes, everything flowed on peacefully. No one was up when I tiptoed out into the garden. It was as yet still very early but light. A heavy dew lay on the grass and made of the leaves around a billion of crystal-points of wonder. Wandering idly, I was content to drink in the beauty and peace of the morning. There was only the happy twitter of birds and the gentle rustling whisper of the leaves that seemed to add to rather than detract from the harmony of this quiet valley.

Leaving the house, I wend my way to that tiny bubbling brook which dances over the stones, laughing and leaping at the secrets it only knows. My whole being drank in the sweet morning fragrance. Here, in a world of dew whose crystal drops beaded more heavily each drooping blade of grass, I had knelt in body and spirit. Here, I guess one could easily forget the petty annoyances and disappointments of life.

But could one forget War? Could one, I wonder.

Returning, I had gathered a posy of the mountain flowers. Those delicate, exquisite blooms, lasting only until the sun got too strong for them. But this morning, poor things, they saw little of the sun as they were crushed and bruised by my hands when upon my ears fell that fateful word, 'War!'

I had met Dad, feeling strong and wholesome in spirit after my morning's excursion to be confronted by his grim face as he announced the news that Singapore was bombed this morning by the Japanese and that this meant we are now at war with Japan.

Bewildered I had uttered that word to myself and looked at my stepmother whose face showed traces of recent tears. Dad then walked away in silence. Vichim, my stepmother, collapsed in a chair and started sobbing—from what? I know not.

All I knew was that I found myself wandering back to my little stream where I stood and only heard the rushing of the waters. Was it trying to tell me something earlier. I wonder.

Then I remembered the blossoms, still clutched tightly in my hands. I looked at them—no longer fresh but lifeless and broken. Dead! The word leapt before my eyes. I let them fall from my fingers into the water and watched them being carried away, away. Gone!

Death! War! Only then did I begin to realise what it meant. Those flowers—some of them only buds, died before serving their time. I had killed them; not thinkingly but it seemed symbolic of what War is. Before me, I imagined deaths and sufferings—all caught in the web of war. And what is war?—a fight for freedom or power? A battle for one's right to peaceful living. War has reared its ugly head here to shatter our peace and we must fight to keep our Peace.

Again I returned to the house. Thoughts revolved inside my head—how best to serve my country.

There was a time I had envied other girls in the services and wished I was one of them. Now here was my chance to do my duty. Suddenly I felt brave and excited at the prospect of having to fight.

Alas! for my high hopes of being useful to my country. When I told Dad of my decision to join up, he promptly told me that I was too young.

'Besides, I'm going to send you back to the convent. You'll be safe there. No! don't argue—I have decided.'

Dad is a strict authoritarian and what he says goes. So, I bowed to his wish, feeling bitterly disappointed.

Dad then received a letter from his company recalling him to work. And so ends our 'Grand Tour'.

We had planned to leave for Australia on the 14th. Instead, we leave here for our home on the mines.

Still, we have till the 14th and I intend to make the most of our stay up here.

This evening before turning indoors, I watched the sun slowly setting behind the mountains. I watched its almost level rays reaching into the valley. The evening light is kindly and soft as I write all this down and promise myself that I must keep a record of everything that is going to happen.

I look towards the stream, gliding and flashing shields of silver and gold where the sun shines on it. I sigh and with Wordsworth I write his lines:

> I heard a thousand blended notes,
> While in a grove I sat reclined,
> In that sweet mood when pleasant thoughts
> Bring sad thoughts to mind.
> To her fair works did Nature link
> The human soul that through me ran;
> and much it grieved my heart to think
> What man has made of man . . .

God's Will be done in all things but I pray Thee keep us from harm Into thy Hands we entrust ourselves and so I prayed.

'As the shades of night are falling fast', I bring this, my first entry, into a new beginning to a close. Goodnight, dear Diary.

14 December 1941   **Sungei Luas, Kampar, Lower Perak**

Phew! What a day! At last we are back home and do I feel tired! We left Renglet this morning. Tears were in my eyes as I silently bade farewell to our holiday home. Wonder how long it will be before I go back there again.

Our departure was uneventful. We had packed last night and the taxi we ordered arrived on time. It wasn't long before we were winding our way down the mountain road to the plains below. A few Sakais were about and stared at us as we whizzed past. The air was cool and fresh. The vegetation, green and undisturbed.

On the main road, after leaving the hills, we saw several lorries of volunteers passing by. We recognised some of our friends from the mines. I wondered where they were going—perhaps to K.L. [Kuala Lumpur] or maybe to Singapore. Nearing Kampar, I heard a most peculiar sound—an unearthly wail which seemed to echo through the air, again and again. That was the first time I heard what Dad called the 'Alert'. What a weird noise and I'm sure I'm not going to like the 'Alert' at all! We had to stop and take cover among the bushes along the road but only for a few minutes. The air was again startled by another sound—The 'All Clear'. I think I prefer this noise to the first one!

In Kampar we stopped at Luan San Store to buy some tinned food. There were two lorries there as well and I saw for the first time, soldiers who appeared tired, unshaven, with their uniforms covered with mud and blood. They did look grim. I stared at them with wonderment of teenage hero-worship! Dad spoke to them and they gave him the latest news of the war—it was not good—the Japs are coming down from the North and the civilians are leaving their homes as the Japs advance.

A few cars roared by—mud-splashed! Then we heard that Ipoh was just bombed and these people were getting out. I saw a young woman with her hair still in curlers . . . She did look funny!

The soldiers were very hungry and as they could not speak the language, made signs indicating that they wanted food and drink. It took them a while to be understood but after many gestures and grimaces they were conducted to a cafe. From afar I looked at them with admiration. I was too shy to go up to them and help them. To me they were men from another planet. Apart from my father, I know little of man and his ways so I guess I wouldn't know what to say if one of them had spoken to me.

We arrived at the mine this afternoon. The place is deserted except for the servants looking after their bosses' houses. The only Europeans left are Dad and the manager.

Trooper, our ugly bulldog and Billy, the fox terrier, greeted us excitedly. They are certainly glad to see us. What are we going to do with them later is going to be a problem.

Tonight we are sleeping in the mosquito room as we are too tired to get the bedrooms organised. We'll be able to listen to the wireless for news now and find out what's happening.

Mum is all scared and worried. As for me—I don't exactly know how I feel. It seems so unreal.

It's so quiet here that I can't believe there's a war on. Of course, we are miles away from the township.

It's early to bed for all of us. The floor's going to be hard but I doubt if that's going to worry us.

Ah Juan, our Chinese boy, was able to fix us a terrific meal. Told Dad I was going to keep a diary. He thinks that's great, provided I can keep it up.

16 December 1941   **Sungei Luas, Kampar**

Went to Ipoh this morning. Was surprised to see the difference war has done to the town in so short a time.

No longer carefree—the people had a nervous, scared look on their faces. Some of the buildings that had been hit looked bleak and unsightly. The shops were still doing business and apart from the scarcity of people about the remains of the buildings that were hit, there was nothing to show that war is here. The day was peaceful and the sun shone in a relentless blue sky.

I called at the Convent and saw Rev. Mother and some of the girls. Quite a few of them had gone home. Rev. Mother told Dad, only those who have no relatives are staying in the Convent. So, that was that. Somehow, I felt glad that I am going to be with Dad. I bade the nuns goodbye, feeling at the same time a little sad for I had been happy with them . . .

Now, I'm going to be out in a world I scarcely know. How will I cope with it? I'm afraid!

Dad, dear Dad—he's the dearest and best in the world but alas! I'm just a girl and he's had so little to do with my upbringing except to see that I'm properly fed, clothed and educated.

If I had been the boy he wanted, what a difference it would have made to him. Thinking of him, I begin to think of my own mother. As always, I wonder who and where she is now. Is she still alive? Why doesn't Dad ever speak of her? And there is a memory that haunts me of a certain woman who had played an important part in my childhood—someone I had called 'Mother' who used to beat me up whenever I was naughty; who had a violent temper. Yet—everything is so confused with so many other memories that crowd unbidden when I think of my childhood.

From what I can remember, my early childhood was not a very happy one— we knew poverty and starvation and unhappiness born of a family not united. It's all so vague now. Only now and again I catch a glimpse of the past and begin to wonder. It's funny how a child invents some things and lives in a world of fantasy—I invented a 'Dream Mother', someone I could talk to in my thoughts— guess I've got some sort of a complex about mothers! Ah, well! Such is life and I must make the best of it!

25 December 1941   **Petaling (Tin Ltd) Kuala Lumpur**

What a Xmas! but the day is quiet—no sirens, planes, or bombs! Nothing disturbs the peace of Xmas today and we celebrated it in a quiet way. Perhaps the Japanese are celebrating the birth of Jesus too!

'Peace on earth, good will to man' etc.

We left Sungei Luas on the 18th and what a journey we had! It was terrifying—at least, to me.

Sungei Luas is tucked away from any town but we could hear very faintly the wail of the siren and if we listened hard enough we could hear the planes and then the bombs.

Dad received his orders to leave for Petaling (another mining township). We packed again. We seemed destined to move from place to place as the war progressed. We chartered a special truck for our heavy luggage. We took only essentials with us to go in the car.

Unfortunately, the driver decided not to leave his home town. This meant we had to travel by train.

At about half past one that afternoon, Dad, Vichim, myself and our two dogs were driven to the station.

On the way we stopped at a store to pick up some food supplies when the siren (now a familiar sound) dismally wailed its warning that raiders were within the neighbourhood. There was a terrific scuttle. Legs were seen vanishing down the streets. Soon the town of Kampar was deserted, save for a few foolhardy souls like us, leisurely strolling to the air-raid shelter which was in the large orchard just outside the town area.

While patiently waiting for the All Clear, there came in the distance the sound of the train. We looked at each other. Dismay was written in Dad's face.

'Whoo-oo-oo' came the welcomed sound of All Clear. We dashed forth with the dogs, got into the car and drove off.

Hope rose in our hearts but that sank as we heard the fateful whistle, signalling that the train was pulling out. Too late! Arriving at the station we were told that there were no more trains that day until three in the morning.

We resigned ourselves to sleeping in the waiting room. Luckily, we had a few things with us . . .

The deepening dusk found us walking up and down the platform. The dogs were restless and unhappy. The hours dragged and when we tried to eat, we found that we were not as hungry as we had thought. The dogs, though, made quick work of their meal.

Sleep was our next thought. I curled myself as best as I could in the armchair while the others found for themselves two long chairs. The dogs whimpered at first but soon settled down.

The desire to turn woke me up from my cat-like position. Dad was not with us. Thinking he had gone out to stretch his legs, I decided to do likewise. Getting up was a stiff task but managed to let myself out without disturbing the remaining occupant.

There was a dim light at one end of the station. As I proceeded further, I stepped into a miserable darkness. Shaking myself, I tried to feel my way around. I stumbled against a hard object. It was one of the benches on the platform. With more courage I continued, my hand on the bench, guiding my way. The air was damp with dew. The whole atmosphere uncannily quiet. I shivered. Suddenly, I touched a human hand. I froze, my heart skipped a beat. 'Who's that?' came a voice out of the darkness. I sighed with relief and answered, 'It's me, Dad'.

He was stretched out on the bench, getting a breath of fresh air as he found the heat in the waiting room was too much for him.

'Listen! I think I can hear the train.' Faintly but clearly we heard the puff-puff-puff of the train. We went to inquire if that was our train. It was.

The approaching train drew nearer and nearer like a monstrous creature, belching smoke and cinders into the night air. Dim lights began to appear on the platform.

At last the monster stood still, panting and blowing out steam. Dark figures suddenly appeared and were seen scrambling into the carriages.

Leaving Mum to look after herself, Dad and I went in search of the guard's van where we could leave the dogs. But we had trouble locating the right carriage in the darkness.

The shrill blast of the whistle warned us that the train was about to leave. I had no time to think as Dad yelled, 'Quickly, get on the tender'.

We managed with some difficulty to clamber up and heaved the dogs after us. Then began a nightmare of a journey as the train slowly gathered speed, freely showering us with soot and sparks. We had got on the tender between the coal truck and the first carriage which we found out was locked. There we sat, huddled together with the trembling dogs between us. I shivered as the rushing of the cold wind stung my face. The train went roaring and dashed headlong into the mysterious and invincible darkness. I shuddered at the thought of what would happen if we fell asleep. There was no fear of that as we grimly clung tightly together.

The dogs quietened down after a while. The train thundered along with alarming rapidity. We prepared to accept the situation with a prayer for our safety. 'Dear Lord, into thy hands, we place our lives.'

The cloud of burning embers descended continually around us. The rush of cold air helped to put most of the glowing sparks out; the only danger was to our eyes, so we kept them closed most of the time. It was a night of suspense!

Suddenly I realised the train was slowing down, then came to a stop. Thinking this was our chance to get off, we lost no time in getting off our precarious perch. Hurriedly we tried to find an opened carriage. Lady Luck was with us. We found one and tumbled into it, dragging the dogs with us. We found ourselves among an assortment of humans and animals. We were told that this was the 'refugee train' from Penang. We managed to squeeze into a corner. Exhausted, I fell into an uneasy sleep.

The sudden lurch of the train woke me up from a terrifying dream. Looking through the window I saw the platform of a station disappearing as the train moved out.

The sky was turning into the pearly grey of dawn. The shadows along the rail tracks no longer looked menacing as they did a few hours ago.

The train stopped at Kuala Lumpur Station at half past nine. We got down, wearily, and went in search of Mum who also had a very uncomfortable journey. The babble and confusion on the platform was simply deafening. Everybody was talking at once. War is certainly a disruption!

We walked away from the crowd. Someone was calling 'Tuan Allan, Tuan Allan?' Dad stopped and raised his hand and answered 'Here!' The Indian driver peered at Dad, saying, 'You are Tuan Allan?' He shook his head as if he didn't believe Dad.

No wonder. When Dad and I looked at each other, we did look a sight! Covered from head to foot with soot, holding onto two dogs in the same blackened state. Some of the crowd stared at us and kept their distance.

Recovering from his surprise, the driver took us in his car and drove us to a hotel first where we had a wash before tucking into some food. Mum had the audacity to laugh at us!

After we had done justice to the meal, we were driven here. The manager greeted us and took us to our new home and here we will be staying—for how long, I wonder.

It's not such a bad place. There's another house a few yards away from us. Our neighbours are a Dutchman and a Scotsman.

The Dutchman is thin and tall with greying hair, a moustache and blue eyes. I don't like him much—don't know why.

The Scotsman, he's nice but likes to drink a lot. I like hearing him talk—the accent is so fascinating.

Then, there's an Australian, an old friend of Dad's. He's short, fat and jolly, in his sixties—he rides the bike like a schoolboy! I like him very much.

Another Dutchman is married to an Eurasian. They are a quiet pair and keep to themselves.

The youngest of our neighbours is William Glennon who is about twenty-five. He is also a Scotsman with a round serious face, brown eyes and hair. Tall and slim and quite good-looking in a way.

29 December 1941

A bus stopped at our place this afternoon because the Alert was on. Imagine my surprise when I saw that they were the Convent people. They were going to Klang Convent with the babies and the rest of the nuns were to follow later. I ran out to the bus and were they surprised to see me too. We talked for a while and when the All Clear sounded we said our goodbyes and the bus took them down the road—away, away! . . .

Our luggage has not arrived yet—hope it's not lost. Dad's going to inquire at the station tomorrow and find out what's happened to the truck.

Nearly every day the Alert is sounded. The planes fly over. There are sounds of the ack-ack firing; in the distance can be heard the bursting of the bombs. What news we hear is not good. Billy and Trooper too have learnt to hide and lie low whenever the Alert is on. Don't know what's going to happen to them when we finally get the order to leave. Guess Dad will destroy them.

Everyone is kind and friendly here. But we don't entertain much. Bill Glennon often comes down to visit us. I'm so shy of people. Wish I could make conversation.

1942

1 January 1942

New Year's Day! Happy New Year—that's a laugh! Wonder what the year will bring—will we still be here next year?

Just imagine I was nearly bound for Australia today. Dad received a note ordering Mum and me to be ready to leave today.

The Company was evacuating the women and children and paying their passage to Australia. I didn't want to go but Dad insisted. Mum, at the last moment, broke down and refused point-blank to leave him. Without realising it she was the means of making me stay too. When the manager found out that she wasn't leaving, he had to send our ticket away to be altered. Consequently I'm left behind. Somehow, I believe it's Fate. I'm glad I'm staying with Dad.

Well, our things are gone. Dad had permission to look in the yard for the truck. To our horror we found the truck broken into and had been looted by the Malays. In fact, two of them were shot by the MPs on duty the night before. All Dad's clothes and his twenty years collections in Malaya had all gone. Mum and I were lucky with regard to clothes. We found them untouched. They must have only wanted men's clothing . . .

There are some soldiers stationed not far from us. We've made a few friends among them. Dad sometimes invites them to a meal and they'd talk late into the night about things that I don't understand. But I like listening.

My favourites are Lieutenant Campbell and his driver, 'Brown Eyes'—don't know his name but he has just about the loveliest pair of brown eyes, heavily lashed. He's only twenty and I believe the others call him 'Brown Eyes' too. Then there's Scotty, a jolly, round-faced Sergeant Major who always has a store of stories about the boys to tell us.

One of his pet yarns is about a batch of boys in Kelantan. The Japs were trying to hit the bridge but failed after several attempts. One of the lads got real excited, jumped up and shouted, 'Hey, drop us a few more and we'll blow the b—— bridge up for you.' Needless to say, the poor boy got pulled down in a hurry!

10 January 1942

The situation is getting worse each day. Dad is in the Demolition Squad and he's blowing up important parts of the dredges. Mum and myself are the only women left on the mines now. Every day we're expecting to get orders to move out. And today the orders came through to get ready—we leave tomorrow. Our friends came to wish us 'Selamat jalan'. I went to Klang Convent to take my last leave of the nuns. With prayers, wishes and tears we parted. Trooper and Billy were going to be destroyed but our Chinese cook-boy offered to look after them and, patting them adieu, they were led away to his home in the nearby kampong. Everything is packed and we are all on edge wondering what next?

12 January 1942

Well, we left Petaling for Singapore yesterday at about 3 p.m. in a convoy of twenty-one. The three of us found ourselves in a car driven by Mr Daniel who foolishly refused a good car—wanted his old one! Our stop for the night was Malacca and on our way there nothing much happened. We passed rubber plantations and saw our soldiers camped there. They waved to us, made the victory sign and were very cheerful.

Arrived safely in Malacca by evening and went to the rest house to spend the night there but unfortunately there was no room. We were nearly arrested and detained for questioning. Explanations over we were allowed to go about our business. We had to go somewhere—anywhere to spend the night. The others pushed on. We stayed behind with Mr Daniel's car. Had left our luggage (the little we have) at the rest house but Mr D kept his in the car boot. We decided to find the others, each of us carrying a small bag of essentials. At last we found them at a Chinese Hotel. We got a room and having satisfied our innards we turned in for the night.

Today our convoy got ready to leave but Mr D found his car had to be fixed up! Seeing we were in his car, we felt we'd stay behind with him. The others went first. Mr D took his car to Borneo Company for repairs. We stayed at the hotel. After tiffin [lunch] we rested in our room when suddenly I heard tramp, tramp, tramp of marching feet!. Rushed to the window, looked out onto the narrow street. What I saw made me feel cold, for below in the street, the Punjabs, guns and vicious looking knives, were marching four abreast. Practice? Oh, no, it didn't look like it. Their faces were hard and grim. The civilians scuttled indoors. Dad said, after silently watching them go by, that it looked as if they were preparing for a land fight. Nothing else could be heard except the crunching of heavy boots on the road. Into the air a voice yelled Dad's name. Looking down we could discern Mr D wildly waving his hands about, shouting to us to hurry down and bring our things. We needed no second bidding. Snatching up our belongings

we raced downstairs, out of the front door and collided into the man himself!
He was about as hysterical as he could be in his explanations that he had heard
the Japs had landed on the coast—hence the army of Punjabs.

'We must leave at once' he cried out and bundled us into his car. Told him
we had some luggage at the rest house but he was impatient to be off and said
there was no time to lose. It was useless to argue with a panic-stricken man.
We left Malacca in a car that hadn't had time to be repaired properly. What
happened was a foregone conclusion.

It wasn't long before the vehicle broke down completely. There we were,
stranded by the side of the highway, enemy planes flying overhead and in the
distance could be bombs being dropped! If the news were true we'll be slaughtered
by the invading Japs. What a thought! I was scared, oh so scared. Dear God,
help us through somehow.

A local lorry thundered along, saw us waving in distress. Stopped and an Aussie
soldier inquired if he could help. We told him of our plight. He offered to tow
us as far as Tampin—their destination. So, in that 'stately fashion' we arrived here.
There were a good many open-mouthed stares as we entered the township. Our
soldier friend—let's call him Harry, is a gunner in the AIF—in his early thirties
and had a wife in Australia, with three kiddies. Said he was in charge of the Tampin
Railway Station and had left Seremban with the nursing staff to Malacca Hospital
but he had not heard about any Japanese landing. So, that was a wild rumour
after all. Dad, I'm sure, felt as if he could have put Mr D across his knees and
spanked him! I certainly felt like it.

While talking to us, an Indian came towards us with a nasty gleam in his eyes
which were blood-shot. Gunner Harry told him quietly to push off but he refused,
so our friend, fixing the bayonet to his rifle strode purposefully towards the fellow.
The Indian hesitated, looked at Harry, measuring him up. My heart stood still
and silently I prayed that there was not going to be a fight. Apparently seeing
sense at last, he turned away, muttering to himself. Harry followed and 'bang'
the shot rang, loud and clear. I nearly jumped out of my skin but he had only
fired into the air. The man took fright and ran down the street as if the very
devil was after him. Harry came back to us with a smile, escorted us to the rest
house where he left us to go back to his post.

Mr D went to the club and got talking to the RAF boys on weekend leave.
Later found ourselves there and got introduced to the boys. We had a sing-song
in the dimly lit room when an elderly gentleman with shrewd looking eyes and
a stern mouth made his appearance. He looked at us without a smile but the
boys just continued to sing. He beckoned to Dad who went outside with him.
Later I asked Dad who the man was. 'OCPD [Officer in Charge of the Police
Department] of the Tampin Police,' I was told and he went on to say that he
was told off in no uncertain terms for not having evacuated Mum and myself.

Dad explained the position and he seemed satisfied—said he was evacuating the police today and offered to take us to Singapore. In a few hours' time once again we shall take to the road. Oh, dear! always on the move it seems—ahead of the enemy each time!

13 January 1942   **Shang Onn Hotel, Beach Road, Singapore**

Here we are in a small room of our own in a small Chinese Hotel after having spent all day looking for a place where we could stay for a while.

It's been hectic—our last part of the journey here. We left late that evening (yesterday) in the police convoy, led by the fire brigade. The lorry of RAF boys and some of the policemen followed, we came next with Mr D driving and a Malay policeman next to him. Our lorry was packed with ammunition. Dad, Mum and I sat at the back with this dangerous cargo. The last to follow was the car with the OCPD and a few inspectors. We did not have a smooth journey, what with the air raids and machine-gunning going every now and again, dodging the planes and hearing the whistle of the bombs before they erupt into terrifying blasts. At one stage of our journey we had to scramble out of our vehicles and take cover into the high gutters at the sides of the road until the enemy planes flew out of sight—it was one time they decided to drop their bombs elsewhere! It was awful wondering if you're going to come out alive and imaginging bombs being dropped right over you. We soon got on our way again. Passed abandoned lorries, cars and buses. The soldiers we passed on the way yelled to us to keep our spirits up—'it won't be long'.

As we were nearing Gemas, we came across a burning car blocking half of the road. We had to keep going and the order was to rush for it and we did just that. I dared hardly breathe and uttered a prayer as our turn came to risk it. The hot, hungry red flames came nearer as we approached the bonfire. I closed my eyes as we drove through and could almost visualise the flames ravenously licking the sides of the lorry with their fiery tongues. There was roaring in my ears, I had difficulty in breathing, my skin prickled with the intense heat and I was so sure that we'd be blown to bits with a tremendous explosion. I was expecting it but nothing happened. I gave a sigh of relief, tears streaked down my cheeks. I looked at Dad and Mum—they too thought the end had come as they clung to each other in their expectancy of the worst.

The ordeal by fire was over. A cool breeze fanned my hot cheeks. We let out a 'whoop' of sheer relief which ended in shuddering sobs of exhaustion.

We stopped at Segamat rest house to have a bit to eat. While there I met a girl I hadn't seen for at least four years. Recognised her instantly although now she's grown taller and ever so much prettier. She could hardly recognise me. She was with her mother. They, too, were trying to get to Singapore. We only had time to inquire how we were and what had we been up to when we were ordered to leave and be on the highway again.

This time the journey was uneventful. Soon it was dark but we continued on our way without another stop. About 11.30 p.m. we arrived in Singapore and went straight to the Police Station. Dad and Mr D stayed the night there while we were taken to the Salvation Army Home. We spent a very restless night and neither of us was happy about staying in the home. When Dad came to see us this morning we asked to be taken away and be with him.

From the time we left the home till now, we three searched for a place to stay. Most of the hotels were full or else they were too scared to take us in—I guess we looked like something the cat dragged in!

However, we struck lucky with this one on our weary travels. They had a vacant room. We took it without bothering to see it. We are right opposite the Volunteers' Headquarters. We discovered that Mr Aussie (that's what I called Dad's Australian friend) has a room here too but he'll be leaving for Australia soon.

16 January 1942
Had been on a shopping expedition. Bought ourselves some clothes. We seemed to be rather unlucky when it came to clothing ourselves. Mr Aussie left two days ago. We had visitors this afternoon. Dad was out. Mum invited them to our room—the only place we could receive anyone.

Bill Glennon had found out where we lived and decided to pay us a call. He introduced us to his friend, Mr Philips (I think that's the name). Anyway, as Bill was going to enter our room, Mr Philips detained him, saying, 'Wait a moment, young man. How long have you known these two ladies?' I smothered a giggle—me? a lady?

'Oh, for about a month,' Bill answered. 'Indeed!' uttered the older man, very astonished. 'You can't enter a lady's room with only a short acquaintance to recommend you. Come! We'll make them receive us elsewhere.' With that we trooped downstairs, ordered ourselves something to eat and drink.

He is nice, that Mr Philips. We talked and talked and talked. Dad came back and we talked some more!

19 January 1942   Rex Hotel, Singapore
'Snatched from the jaws of death' as it were! That's exactly what happened yesterday. All I can say is that our ticket can't have been on that bomb—or else I wouldn't be writing this down.

Dad was with us—he had decided not to go out that morning. So, there were Dad, Mum and I just sitting in our room doing nothing—just waiting, waiting and waiting . . .

When the air raids were on and we had plenty each day, we went down to the 2nd floor under the staircase for shelter. From our room we can hear the warning whistle from the roof spotter on the VHQ before the official wail of the siren is sounded. The first and second raids came and went. Bombs were exploding in the distance. There we were, crouched under the staircase, our hearts beating rapidly and our thoughts running wild—will we come through this one and so on it goes.

The All Clear whistle from the spotter was heard. We got out from under the shelter and proceeded upstairs to our room. Of course, the official All Clear hadn't sounded yet.

On our way up I heard the droning of the planes (I have already learnt to know the sound of the bombers) approaching nearer and nearer. There was no warning whistle but it could have been given and we failed to hear it. Something prompted me to return to the shelter. I shouted to Dad and Mum to come down. Dad said the All Clear whistle had gone and he heard no warning signal. I grew frantic and yelled for them to come down at once. They hesitated, then thought better of it when the planes drew nearer and the ack-ack guns started firing.

We reached the shelter just in time as the first bomb was dropped. We flung ourselves flat on the floor and whizz-shiss-ss-ss, crr-crr-rump, crash came the bombs one after another. I heard the whistling of each of them as they hurtled down from the sky and waiting for the rest—the explosion—to follow. The building rocked beneath us. An orange flame from a bursting bomb flashed in a downward streak as it passed an open window. Screams of human fear and pain penetrated through the sound of the crashing force of the bombs. Smoke and acrid smell assailed us through cracked and open windows. There was dust everywhere. Mum had her head buried in her arms, sobbing. Dad had his arms around her. I, for that split second closed my eyes and thought 'this is it!' The danger had passed—no sounds of planes or firing. The 'All Clear' rang through our fuddled minds as we lay on the floor, shaken and white-faced. The raid was over and we are alive!

We got up, rather dizzily, dusting ourselves and feeling ourselves all over to ascertain if any bodily damage had been done. No, we were safe and sound in limb and body. Mentally and emotionally, I'm not sure. I think I grew old, very old and very frightened during that short time when I had my face down on the floor!

We made our way through the debris of plaster, splinters, broken furniture and dead bodies—poor souls, they hadn't reached the shelter in time. Dust, smoke, foul-smelling fumes seemed to fill the atmosphere as we choked and gasped for a breath of fresh air which was non-existent!

It was too much for Mum. She was on the point of collapse as we helped her upstairs.

When we got to our room which was facing the VHQ we stared into a wreck of a room. There was a huge hole in the ceiling. The floor was littered with pieces of armoury, broken wooden frames, broken glass and brickwork. Dad picked several pieces of the metal, turning them over in his hands. He reckoned that they must have come from the dump of machinery outside the Headquarters. Our windows and walls were no longer as such and if we had stayed in the room—well, it would have been 'Kingdom come' for us three. Mum became hysterical at the state of the room and refused to stay another day there, so off once again we went seeking somewhere else to stay.

Dad went across to hand over the metal he had picked up. When he came back he announced that we've had a very lucky escape as there were two bombs lying not fifty yards away—unexploded! Duds perhaps! Whew! Certainly we weren't meant to die—not yesterday anyway!

Beach Road was closed to us so we decided to go through North Bridge Road. We came upon the dead and dying. Many were badly injured. Ugh! it was awful seeing them lying around uncovered with blood that was still warm and from some, the blood seemed to flow steadily on, making a pool of red. In fact, crimson seemed to be the dominant colour. No matter where we looked our eyes rested on dead bodies, dying people—men, women and children and so many of them with horrific injuries. How could I describe such a scene? I've never read of such things, let alone seen them before now. I can't find the right words to convey the pitiful sight of this human life ebbing away; of the useless loss of life; of the young children crying either in pain, fear or loss; of the agony some of them must have felt and are still suffering. What a tragedy.

So, this is War! This is what War does! Dear God! What a waste of life! What devastation! A destroyer of the young and old! Who wants to glorify War? Why do we have to fight and hurt each other? So many thoughts go through my mind as I look around me. It is so senseless. No longer am I a happy-go-lucky child but a frightened, uncertain girl of seventeen whose life before had been serene, innocent and joyous. No I am stripped of my sensitive covering—I feel naked—I have no place to hide my tearful face, my knowledge of the evil that has erupted in this world that I am born into. I want to take flight from all this—I don't want to know that this is happening but where do I go? Oh, Lord, help me to understand.

My stomach gave a lurch as I stumbled across an old woman. She was dying, blood oozed from her head and mouth. One leg was doubled under her; her innards were laid open in the sunlight and flies were already feasting on them. One of her arms was missing. What a picture to remember! Her eyes stared at me. I tried to close them but the lids kept retracting. I shuddered—the smell of burnt skin was getting to me. I must have looked pretty green as a cup of steaming black coffee was pressed to my lips. I gulped down the hot fluid and felt the burning sensation go down my throat. It brought me around. I felt better and thanked the young Chinese man in his brass helmet—he was one of the MAS [Medical Aid Service]. They were here, there and everywhere, helping the people, dead and alive. Poor Mum was suffering from the same feeling. She was being helped by another MAS.

We managed to get away from the bombed area after what seemed like hours. We found our way to Robinson's where we met a European who insisted we eat something, then offered to take us back to the hotel in his car. We returned only to pack the little we had and with his help we found a flat in Middle Road owned by a Jewess.

We stayed there last night—there were no more raids but something else happened. There was an old man with snow-white hair staying there too and we invited him to have a drink with us and pass away the evening together. There we were, the four of us, sitting and talking about everything in general and nothing in particular. The light in our room was too bright for the brown-out regulation so I went to shade it with a navy blue material round the globe—a silly, stupid thing to have done, I now realise. It seemed all right and went on talking. A while later I glanced upwards and noticed smoke issuing forth. I yelled to Mum to switch off the light as the cloth began to smoulder. We tried to take it off but it was too late. The shade burst into flames and 'bang' went the globe. Dad seized a cushion and began beating out the light fire the explosion caused. The room was filled with an awful odour. We had to hurriedly open all the windows. The old man went out and brought back a small shaded lamp. With the help of a torch I looked for pieces of glass from the globe. We continued then with our conversation. None of us felt like sleeping but finally the party broke up. I tried to get some sleep—eventually dropped off and dreamt of horrible, gory mess—I might as well have stayed awake!

Today we took shelter in the Cathay Building when we got caught in the air raid. Then we had lunch at the Rex Hotel. Saw the manager, an old friend of ours. He fixed a room for us. Back to the flat to pay what was due for the night's lodgings plus the broken globe and shade. For the time being we'll be staying at the hotel.

28 January 1942   **Rex Hotel, Singapore**
On the road to recovery—I have been ill with the diarrhoea my temperature shot up to 103°. Dad wanted to put me in hospital but I refused to go—I didn't even want to stay in bed! Two days later, coming downstairs I began to feel faint. Someone was coming up the stairs and next thing I knew I was being picked up and taken to the lounge. The young man who came to my aid fetched the

manager who went and got Dad. A consultation was held and the outcome?—
The manager gave me his unoccupied room on the ground floor for safety and
it was also convenient as the toilet was next door. I took residence there. It was
sure safe enough. There was a large table with four mattresses on it and me lying
on top of two more. Sandbags were stacked up all around the table. I had food
brought up to me—a diet consisted mainly of water and condensed milk. I lapped
it all up greedily! Having a constitution of an ox I didn't take long to recover.
Now I'm back upstairs in our room. While downstairs I heard very little of what
was happening—in any case, I didn't care as I was too sick to bother much about
what went on.

1 February 1942   **Rex Hotel, Singapore**
Went to the passport office today. There were crowds of people about. Gosh!
the city looks a wreck. Soldiers everywhere.

We were not in the building very long when the raiders came over and did
their usual stuff. The building shook with the blast. The sight within the building
was somewhat laughable—people scurried every which way, like a disturbed line
of ants! Legs sticking out from under tables and chairs. Some just dropped flat
on their tummies with hands clasped over their heads. Others found refuge in
cupboards! The raid didn't last long. The office resumed its duties as if nothing
happened—everything went on as usual until the next scramble for safety!

Yesterday we found a house 'To let' near the aerodrome. Went to have a look
at it—talk about luck! We arrived there to discover that it had been bombed the
day before.

On our way back we met Bill who was pleased to see us. We made some
friends among the soldiers who often dropped by for drinks at the Rex. Some
of them are young and cheeky, wanting to kiss me at every opportunity—I'm
not sure how I'm supposed to react to such goings on. Guess it's not something
I indulge in.

There are also two planters staying here—Mr M who is in his forties, thin with
receding hairline and large intense brown eyes. He moves quickly and makes
me feel uncomfortable as I never know when I'm going to bump into him—one
minute he's at your side, next he's standing behind you. Sometimes when he
looks at me, I feel like throwing a towel or something over his head. For some
reason I feel nervous with him about—It's a feeling I'm not sure I like having.

The other fellow, Mr A, is nice. He's quiet. Goes about his business. He towers
over me. His greying hair needs cutting. His blue eyes twinkle at you under bushy
eyebrows which move up and down in rapid succession as he talks—a nervous
habit, maybe? Anyway, I like him better than Mr M who seems to glower at me

whenever I chose to sit next to Mr A. Who cares? Not I 'said the sparrow' with a giggle!

3 February 1942   4 Amber Mansions, Orchard Road, Singapore
It wasn't safe to stay at the Rex any longer. Once more we moved out and came here. Amber Mansions is a group of flats in Orchard Road. Mrs C the owner of No 4 is leaving for Australia in a couple of days. She decided to leave the flat and everything in it to us for the sum of $350. Of course, we took it. It's not a bad place. There are four room (bedrooms) and both Mr M and Mr A came to stay with us—just like one big family!

There is a piano in the lounge room. We found out that Mr M is quite a musician.

Our air-raid shelter is under the stairs on the ground floor. It is quite a good one and opens out onto the backyard of the Mansions. As far as we know, we're the only ones in the building. If there are others, then they must keep to themselves all the time as we haven't seen or heard anybody else about.

12 February 1942   Amber Mansions
What a life! What a day! I'm writing this in the shelter just after our third raid. Mrs Christie left for Australia a couple of days ago. We found an old lady, Mrs Kate, next door and she stays with us now. She told us she was to be evacuated with a group of European women and children—well, they left and forgot to take her with them!

We also have a batch of REs [Royal Engineers] stationed in the grounds. They are here for an indefinite period and are very good to us. Often cooking us meals when we haven't been able to go up to our flat to do so. Our special friend is their cheery, happy-go-lucky cook—the boys call him 'The Boss'. The bombing and shelling is getting worse each day. Last night the firing was so bad from Fort Canning which is situated on a hill directly behind the Mansions that I had to leave my room and make do under the settee in the dining room.

We had some of the soldiers to dinner and they brought us plenty of tinned stuff. During dinner, there was a sharp 'crack' overhead. It made us jump but we couldn't see anything. Not long after that there was another and sharper 'crack'—our blackout paper from the doors and windows gave way and we heard the shell fire—apparently the force of the blast caused the crackling sound of the paper being torn apart. The shelling got worse and worse. It was so bad we decided to go down and sleep in the shelter.

This morning we saw that the flat next-door had been hit. Went up to ours wondering what we would find. I went to my room—imagine my horror when

I saw an ugly looking piece of shrapnel resting on my pillow. Gingerly I picked it up, showed it to Dad and told him where I had found it. It was heavy and jagged-looking—I shudder to think what might have been if I had slept in my bed. I'm going to keep it as a souvenir—a reminder to thank God for my life.

Looks as if we'll be living in the shelter for most of the time. The boys seem to be always cheerful and keep our spirits up with their jokes and stories. Mr M is looking like a scared rabbit these days. I do wish he'd stop sticking so close to me. Once he tried to put his arms around—to 'protect' me he said. I retorted 'I can look after myself, thank you' and moved out of his reach. I don't like him—he makes me feel—oh, I don't know what I really feel—sort of uneasy feeling. All I know is that I don't like him touching me.

15 February 1942   **Amber Mansions**

The shelling is getting from bad to worse. It goes on all day and night. We could see billows of smoke rising from the bombed city of Singapore. Now and again flames would shoot high into the sky—from the oil tanks, I guess. Fort Canning looks ablaze most of the time—we sure are in their direct line of firing! Last night our soldier friends came to tell us that the Japs are advancing and we are retreating! Bad news all round. Then we were ordered to go up to our flat. Imagine our surprise when we discovered our soldiers and the Punjabs stationed all along the stairway with their rifles and bayonets out in readiness for action. It was dark going up and we had to keep shouting 'Civilians coming up!' Stumbling against each other we managed at last to reach our flat and ranged ourselves in the dining room. There is an ominous feeling that something is going to happen.

Mrs Kate became hysterical. Mr M started being silly and romantic (if that is the word to describe his pawing). I tried to quieten Mrs Kate while at the same time kept telling that horrible man to leave me alone.

All the time the shelling continued on both sides. One of them burst overhead. We were thrown off our balance. The plaster came down, half-burying us. It was impossible to stay here any longer. We decided to risk it and return downstairs. Once again yelling at the top of our voices, 'Civilians coming down' we nervously made our way down.

At one stage while helping Mrs Kate down, Mr M grabbed me. I ducked and hit my head against the stone balustrade. Fortunately, I did not knock myself out though my head hurt a bit. Steadying myself I continued my way down with Mrs Kate. As for Mr M—I lost sight of him. Thank goodness!

Arrived at the shelter without further mishaps. Found a space kept for us by the thoughtful Sergeant who seemed to have expected us back. Mum and Dad weren't there and I became worried. The 'Boss' assured me that they'd be all right. Mrs Kate fell into a tired sleep. As for me, sleep was impossible. I kept hearing the heavy drone of the bombers approaching—will they never stop?—they get closer and closer, then the whistling sound as the bombs come hurtling down from the sky. I held my breath, tensed myself for the explosion that followed. Sounds of the ack-ack guns mixed with the noise of the bursting shells overhead—I think those sounds will forever linger in my mind. Every now and again amid the crunching noise of buildings being blown, I heard screams of fear and pain as if some animals were badly hurt in traps. I realised those animals were human beings, myself included, as involuntarily I let out screams of terror as I felt the building shake. Raid after raid—bombs exploding and the continued shelling. Dear God—when is it going to end or is this the end?

Suddenly a man staggered into the shelter. It was Mr M covered in plaster. He 'plonked' himself beside me. The it all began again, wanting to kiss me and saying he loved me. I shifted my position and went to sit next to 'Boss' who told him to leave me alone. He sulked at that. Muttered something about dying being the best way out for him!

This afternoon we received the good news that we had driven the Japs back. Everyone in the shelter gave a mighty cheer. An Irish Sergeant then quietly said, 'Please don't be too happy—the danger is not over yet. Far better to be calm and steady, taking any good news as it comes; likewise the bad ones. Let us rejoice by all means but not too extreme. We must also be prepared for the worse if it comes.'

10.30 p.m. Surrender! the Fall of Singapore

We have surrendered to the Japs. It happened at 8.30 p.m.

We were in the shelter all day. When evening came, it brought in about half-dozen injured soldiers—their injuries were slight but enough to put them out of action for the time being. No one spoke much as we listened to the shells as they whizzed overhead. The terrific burst of them deafened our ears and rendered it impossible to carry on a normal conversation. When we did talk it was mostly about the boys, lying in there with us. We asked them about their lives before the war. They seemed eager to discuss their home life, their families, their sweethearts and what they were going to do when all this 'hell' is over.

About 7 p.m. I heard someone calling for Mrs Kate. I spoke out for her as she seemed to be in a state of shock. Standing at the entrance of the shelter was the figure of a tall man in uniform. He said he was 'Leslie' from the Gordons and wanted to know if Mrs Kate was okay. Then he said a strange thing, 'There won't be any more fighting tonight'. With that he left before we could recover ourselves to ask him what he meant by that remark. We learnt later that he came from Fort Canning. At a quarter to ten we heard an officer commanding his men to line up. Not long after, one of them came with the shattering news, 'We've given up!' 'Boss' came in, dazed-looking. His face working up as if he wanted to cry. He kept repeating to himself, 'I can't understand it—it's not true. We were told we were pushing them back. I can't—' tears ran down his cheeks. He sat down and unashamedly buried his face in his hands and wept as if his heart would break. We tried to comfort him but what was the use—what words could we say. We, too, felt like sobbing our hearts out. There are no words to describe how I felt; how any of us feel! Shocked, disbelief, horrified, anger perhaps. Then there's fear as to what is going to happen. All at once, everybody started talking—trying to convince ourselves that this nightmare is not true.

The firing has ceased. The night air was no longer shattered by the bursting bombs and shells. In fact, the silence is quite frightening. For the first time in weeks, there was no throbbing droning of the planes; no sirens; no guns. I found this silence from the artillery fire more threatening and unnerving to say the least. It gave me the creeps to realise that this is 'Surrender!' We slowly trekked upstairs to our flat with some of the boys. 'Boss' came up later with their stores saying, 'You—you better have these instead of those yellow dogs'. We stayed talking a while. One of them spied the piano. 'Who can play?' he asked. I answered, 'Mr M'. They pushed him on the piano stool and started to sing 'Rule Britannia'. Mr M soon picked up the tune on the piano. Everyone started to sing. It seemed weird that—here we were—capitulated into Japanese hands—singing song after song till we were hoarse. Somehow, drinks were found and poured out. Someone shouted, 'To the King and us.' We drained our glasses and became silent, so silent that one would have heard a pin drop. We were deep in thoughts when 'Boss' made the first move, 'Come on lads, let's out of here. These good folk need sleep and so do we.' With that they left, wishing each other good-night.

16 February 1942

This morning we woke up feeling quite fresh after a night free from bombs and shells. I wonder if our boys had any sleep or did they stay awake, thinking! The Japs are still marching in, on foot and riding on tanks. From our balcony window we saw them yelling, singing and shouting in their triumph. What's going to be our Fate now? I felt fear as I've heard about the Japanese brutality and the atrocities they had done in Shanghai and elsewhere. People had been shot for no reason except that they were there at the wrong time. And the women population—are we going to be safe from them? Who knows! Dad decided to go into town. I went with him. We passed the Rex, saw a whole group of people drinking themselves silly to drown their despair at the news of the surrender. There were ruins all over the place. Part of the Convent was bombed. We heard that our water supply had almost run out, the toilet facilities were almost nil and of course

My father, John Charles Allan, in Malaya.
I think he was in his early thirties when
this photo was taken.

Vichim, my stepmother, before the war.

Malaya before the war. Dad in the centre.

November 1940. I was a schoolgirl at Ipoh Convent. Little did I realise what the following years would have in store.

Mary Winters performing the Fan Dance as part of the concert presented by the Women's Section, 9 January 1943. Mary was fifteen when interned. (Copy of an original print)

The piece of shrapnel found on my pillow, 12 February 1942. The original piece is still in my possession.

there is the ever-present danger of an epidemic if care is not taken in using what water is left.

The sight of Japanese soldiers patrolling the streets kept many indoors. Bodies were being collected by relatives and quickly removed from the scene. Talk about a disaster area! Buildings had fallen on people who never got to the shelter. The continual bombing left the roads looking like volcanic craters. The anti-aircraft guns had finally ceased to fire. We heard Sir Shenton Thomas [Governor of Singapore] speak. The Japanese soldiers were standing beside him as he spoke, telling the population of Singapore to stay off the streets and to be calm; European civilians were to go to Raffles Hotel for registration. We passed streams of our boys. They showed us the 'V' sign. As we came near the Supreme Court we saw a large number of civilians standing around. We inquired what was happening and were told that it was for registration. We gave our names and met some of Dad's friends. Met Leslie again. He came back with us to the Mansions. On our way back we met pals of his and they advised to put Mum and myself in the Convent for safety.

We arrived at the flat to find Mr M crying and drinking. Mum said he had been drinking ever since we left this morning. Silly man! When he saw Leslie he seemed to sober up and glared at our young friend. Later I found out he was insanely jealous of Leslie whose company I found oddly comforting. He's about 24—tall, dark and quite good-looking. I like him very much. I think he likes me too. This seems to make Mr M more jealous. But as much as I like the young man, I was unprepared for what came after.

When it was time for him to leave, I went to the door to see him off the premises. He took me aside, quietly asked me if I'd consider marrying him! I gaped at him. It was so unexpected. It made me draw my armour of reserve closer round me. I was unable to say anything as I tried to collect my thoughts together. He went to say that if I married him, the Japs wouldn't assault me. Another one trying to protect me! He looked so strong and dependable standing in front of me and holding my hands. His face serious and concerned for my welfare. It made me feel—well—sort of shy, I suppose. All I could do was to shake my head and said, 'No, Leslie, I can't marry you. I'm sorry. I don't really want to be married.'

He smiled at that. 'I'm sorry too but marriage would give you some measure of protection. I'll be leaving soon.' He bent down and gently kissed me goodbye. Before I could say anything else he had disappeared down the stairs. I felt a little sad to see him go and it was a nice gesture on his part. I turned around. Mr M was glaring at me.

'What did that man want with you?' he swayed towards me.

'Never mind what he wanted' I retorted back and turned to leave.

He caught my hand, hissing angrily, 'I hate him, I hate him. I'll kill him for taking you away from me.'

I laughed in disbelief and suddenly felt like taunting him. 'Don't be a goat! Leave me alone. I don't like you!'

Pulling my hand out of his grasp I ran out of the room and joined the others. He burst into tears and said that he loved me and I was being cruel to him. Dear, oh dear! I suppose I am but he gives me the creeps and all that 'pawing' Brr-rr how I hate that!

17 February 1942   **Amber Mansions**

I saw our soldiers going on their way to the concentration camp at Changi. Waved to them. They shouted back 'Keep your chins up'—'It won't be long' we heard someone else say. Saw our soldier friend amongst them. We gave him a wave. They looked so brave, marching and singing. I had tears in my eyes—looked at Dad—he stood straight and tall but tears were running down his cheeks. I went to him. His arms came around me—so tightly that I could hardly breathe. No words were spoken.

Now the soldiers are out of the way, the civilians are going to be rounded up next—sounds like a herd of cattle! Military police everywhere—orders given that we must bow from the waist whenever we see them!

Internment began for most of the Europeans today—Europeans mean 'married to one'—'children of such union'—or if you profess to be a 'British subject'!

Very hot this morning—told to be at the Cricket Ground. Dad still wanted to put Mum and self in the Convent so we stayed back at the flat. Mr M left us to work in the Municipal Building. Later Dad and I went out to get some news—it was hopeless—there were others in the same boat—nobody knew exactly what was going to happen.

We found our way to the Central Police Station—had to pass Jap sentries posted along the bridge. They were beating Chinese women and men who wanted to cross it.

The police station was crowded—people clamouring, yelling everywhere—the smell of sweat was overwhelming!

Saw a Jap captain—told us not to worry and to stay in the house until further notice. Returned home but at the bridge the sentries allowed Dad to pass but roughly pushed me back—felt a prick of the point of a bayonet in my back. Guttural sounds came from the man's throat as he thrust the bayonet forward and kept pushing me along. I was petrified and called out to Dad—who tried to explain that I am his daughter. The sentry refused to allow me to pass so we went back to the police station to ask the Jap captain for assistance. He sent an Indian interpreter. Still we were refused permission to pass—only Dad could go. Back again to the captain. This time he sent a Jap soldier to accompany us. The sentry, scowling, replied that no young, unmarried girls should be seen out in the open! The soldier explained why I was out and most reluctantly he let us pass. Phew!

Plenty of Japs living in the empty flats—seem friendly enough and sure make themselves at home when they pay us a visit!

Dad still wants me in the Convent but Mrs K said it would be better if I stayed with them—so it's settled, thank goodness!

26 February 1942   **Amber Mansions**

Dad and Mr A went out yesterday. Returned afternoon with news that they had succeeded in obtaining passes from the Japanese Envoy who told them that we could be interned with these passes in Changi. Told to take enough for ten days, also enough clothes for those ten days.

Dear God! I am scared for all of us. Everything's packed—now we wait!

28 February 1942   **Katong House**

At last! Interned and what trouble we had to get ourselves here. Started off early yesterday morning—a young Jewess told us her brother would drive us to Changi . . . It was a small car and there were six of us! Stopped several times on the way by the Jap soldiers but allowed us to go on when shown our passes. First went to Seaview—no result—only men civilians at the police station. After reading our passes a Jap sentry said to proceed to Changi. Came to the last barricade— the sentries told the men could go, not the women. Luckily an officer came and brought us to Changi Prison—on our way in we saw our soldiers working in the sun—they waved to us and were promptly yelled at by their guards! We were taken to the officer in charge who asked endless questions—often the same ones. Waited for three solid hours! At last action! We were going to be put in Changi Prison—then they changed their minds and took us back to Katong and stopped at the police station again! Here, we were told to get out—'pushed' out more like it! Had our things searched for radios, cameras and any other items of interest to them. Took my tin hat and camera. Saw the shrapnel and inquired where it came from so I said 'Your shell hit our place and nearly killed me'. 'Solly' they said and laughed—'Very funny, solly', and laughed again! But I was allowed to keep it.

Waited for nearly seven hours by the roadside while the officials worked out what was going to happen to us. At half past eight a Jap sentry came along, took the men to the station and we were taken to a house not far away. A huge man admitted us in—saw figures sleeping on the floor. Gave our names—given some food—had had nothing to eat or drink since eight that morning. A very disturbing, uncomfortable night.

This morning saw crowds of women and children milling around. Learnt what it's like to queue for food and stuff! Later we were taken to another house as there was no room for us in the first house—the next and the next—no go! Finally we were taken into the 'White' house as it is called. A thin elderly woman came to our assistance and found us a room for the three of us. Were told there are about 500 women and children together in these houses. Large houses with lots of gardens around. Odd areas are wired off—probably with land mines—these areas are, of course, off limits!

5 March 1942   **Katong House**

What a life! Mosquitos terrible! Our latrines stink! Have to empty 3 times daily in holes dug in the garden. Each of us are given special chores—mine is digging holes to bury the rubbish with Mrs CB helping me. Had a meeting this morning—told could be leaving within the next twenty-four hours for Changi Goal. To have everything packed and ready to go—no ifs or buts!

Sunday, 8 March 1942   **Changi Prison**

Well, we are going after all—everything packed. Hustle, bustle, hither, thither—everyone dashing around and getting nowhere fast! Children crying, women shouting, orders given—nobody takes much notice—nobody seems to know really what's going on—just a mad scramble trying to get organised! Given three tins of sardines and two loaves of bread. We walk to Changi Gaol. (Approximately 8 miles away)—only the very sick, the very old and the very young are allowed to be taken in lorries.

Marching orders set for 11 a.m. and to carry only what is necessary, leaving heavier baggage to follow in the lorries later—much, much later!

Left Katong Camp in the true 'British spirit'—singing along the hot, dusty road—whatever each of us felt inside was disguised by our cheerfulness and in spite of what awaited us at the end of our pilgrimage, we kept our heads and spirits up. Ah! it takes a lot to daunt the 'British spirit'!

The sun, today, seemed more merciless as it shone down on us from a clear, cloudless, still-less sky. Some of us were pretty tired and quite a few just sat by the side of the road, too exhausted to move, even when prodded by the Jap sentries. Eventually, as they were left behind, they were rescued by the passing lorries and a few cars.

At last, here we are—tired, hot and dirty from the dusty road, hungry and very, very thirsty we slowly dragged our feet through those iron gates—glad to see the end of the road. Saw Dad and some of the men standing in the courtyard of the prison.

The iron gates clanged shut as we trooped through. Inside, there are rows and rows and irons stairs to the cells—imagine 9' × 12' cell with a concrete slab in the middle—that's our bed and who's the lucky one to get to sleep on it? We drew lots to see which of us sleeps on the slab. Mum had the honour of being the lucky one—I took one side of the slab and Mrs Kitts had the other space. For toilet purposes there is this Chinese lavatory or 'squatters' at one end. The walls are high and above the slab a tiny window with bars across—could be about 10' above the slab. You wouldn't want to be claustrophobic here or you'd go raving mad!

Outside the cell the walkways sound pretty awful—clang, clang, clang—I swear I can even imagine there are sounds of chains too—the iron stairways are just as noisy as there seem to be endless going up and down those stairs!

The March

E'er the sun was up for one to see
What sort of a day it promised to be—
There gathered a crowd
Of women and children proud!

The children, the sick and the mothers-to-be
Were taken in lorries—one, two, three!
Leaving behind that three hundred
Waiting with hearts unafraid ...
Thus for the Red, White and Blue
This march they had to do.
And they certainly did it
With that British Spirit—
As children of the Flag would do
If they love that Red, White and Blue!

(There! my first attempt at poetry writing—not perfect but my own composition.)

10 March 1942   **Cell 36–A3**

First General Meeting held in the Carpenter's Shop. Didn't know there are so many women interested in running and organising of our camp. Dr Elinor Hopkins was elected Liaison Officer and Camp Commandant. Miss Josephine Foss became our First Floor Representative on A3.

Chores for everyone and changes in roster every fortnight. Men allowed (under guard) to come over to help with the heavier work. The men and women are separated by the courtyard. Menu stinks! Rice and water—called 'bubu'—tasteless and looks like dishwasher water. Porridge, maybe twice a week. Bread or buns every second day if you are lucky. Rations consist of about five sardines, a quarter tin of bully beef with a half a dozen tins of soup to feed about 300—Some diet!!! Any extras of sugar and salt—I must carefully save for emergencies. Now the men have taken over the cooking and that helps quite a bit to boost our morale.

19 March 1942

Miss Foss' birthday—had a little party for her on our floor. Each floor has its own doctor now—ours is Dr Jeanette Robinson. LMO [Lady Medical Officer] is Dr Helen Worth.

There are now over three hundred women and children in our camp. The men have been cooking our meals for a week but now a kitchen has been built and we do our own cooking for the whole camp. I help with the early morning teas and also the first drain sweeper in A Block. The men still come to help with the heavier tasks but we are not allowed to talk to them—the Jap sentries always accompany them.

One of the things we have to learn is to bow to the Japs whenever we see them. Heaven help us if we forget—a clout on the head, a bayonet threateningly thrust in front of you or even a kick on the backside that could send you sprawling onto your face—so, don't forget to bow-wow-wow!!! And no whisperings please or to gather in groups is also a no-no!

29 March 1942

A 'Drain Squad' has been formed. Mrs 'Stiffy' White, the head and I'm her second in command. Hospital on the men's side near the entrance. Our office faces the courtyard—a sentry is always on guard!

Dr Cecily Williams is our dietitian. Dr Robinson and Dr Elliot for the adults in the dispensary—a cell in E Block Lower. Dr Margaret Smallwood for the children and babies and Mrs Farrer helping her. Tea servers—Mrs Dorothy White and Violet Aitken. It takes me all my time to get to know them—at least I can write down their names and that helps.

14 April 1942

Saw Dad yesterday. Being Easter Sunday—only children of seventeen and under were allowed—for an hour. Had no service but I think the Japs will allow soon. Beginning to know a number of people—what a wonderful opportunity to study them—so many different characters—like in a storybook and what lessons you can learn from them!

Mrs Mulvany, a Canadian, is now starting a Red Cross Corner for our benefit. Mrs Freddy Bloom has started a weekly paper called the Changi Pow-Wow. Showers start at half past seven in the mornings and half past eight at nights and you have the sentries as spectators every now and then. Lights out at 10 p.m. Silence hours—2.30 p.m. to 3.30 p.m.—siesta time! and from 10 p.m. to 7.30 a.m. General Meetings to be held in the Carpenter's Shop end of every month. A cheeky fellow by the name of Dan Nicholson has won Mum's favour!

20 April 1942

The Emperor's Birthday! Wow! We were ordered to face towards the sun at 10 o'clock with 'two minutes' silence! When it was ended there were sounds of chains being pulled!!! As a special treat we were given a tin of pineapple to every three women and a box of Rinso to be shared between four women. Some celebration!!!

20 May 1942   Cell 41–A4

Life is still the same old routine. The men have taken over our cooking—the place looks more cheerful. Had a difference with Mrs Kitts and came up here. Diet still terrible and suffering from the effects of my first illness in January. Was carted off to hospital three weeks ago—how I hate hospitals. But Dr Worth very nice and so are the sisters but still I was most anxious to come out. Dad came to see me about three times while in hospital. We had a Red Cross Concert on 2nd May. It was a great success. I did a recitation and a dance. Mrs Angela Kronin arranged it all—what style—what talents—Hollywood style no doubt!

26 May 1942

Miss Foss asked me if I could help Lady Heath who is going to have a baby sometime in July. For Miss Foss I would do anything.

We now have Church Service every Sunday and confession once a month for the Catholics but a Jap sentry is always on guard.

Bowing to the Japanese has become an art with a few sly variations—so far we haven't been caught! The Red Cross is doing well—Sales day on Tuesdays.

Had the first concert arranged by Mrs Betty Milne—I played the mouth-organ—it was a good show. Miss Parfitt—A genius with her sketches.

30 May 1942

Changi School in operation in the dining room—now called the Schoolroom.

Mrs Betty Milne, the headmistress. Other teachers—Griffith-Jones, Rand, M. Robinson and Jean Summers, Mrs Blackman, Eisinger and Mackenzie.

Having nothing to sleep on except a little rug lent to me by Miss Sharman.

Am attracted to Dr Hopkins—I think she's beautiful—grey hair, blue eyes that can look straight through you and a smile that lights up her face. I keep thinking I wish she is my mother—how I'd like my mother to be—my Dream Mother, of course—a dream image I've always had of my own mother.

Our Head Camp Commandant is Lieutenant Okasaki—he reminds me of a peacock when he struts up and down on inspection days. However, he seems to like the children a lot—that's something in his favour, I suppose. As for the rest of the sentries—they can be pigs sometimes—no, most times. Often we would be slapped or given a kick in the bottom if we don't bow correctly or caught whispering!

19 June 1942

French, shorthand, Dutch and Spanish classes have been started. Also girls' club— Changi Club where we have dancing, cooking, first-aid and netball. The concerts are getting better. We now have a piano.

We are getting mince meat (meat, what meat?) three times a week.

Still helping Lady Heath—she's a nice lady. Miss Foss is another nice lady and very highly thought of over the men's Camp. Our hospital is now in our own camp and a sanatorium (of sorts) is being built in A garden.

The men were allowed to give us a concert in the courtyard—it was an instrumental solo concert. Miss Parfitt, Chairman of the Entertainment Committee, has made great strides towards having concerts arranged for future dates—already on the agenda—two Fair dates; one Men's Quartet; Four lectures and the Handicrafts classes plus our own entertainments—hats off to a committee doing such a wonderful piece of work for the camp.

23 June 1942

Parcels are allowed between the two camps but no notes of any sort. Rumours are rife. News somehow gets filtered through—how no one knows and no one is telling!

Not feeling too good today—tummy upset—early hours of the morning. Went to the Doc—temp up, vomiting, diarrhoea—diagnosis—dysentery and in hospital and in isolation. Gripping pains, blood in stools—feel weak, real weak—mustn't faint—hang on, hang on—oh, God, I feel as if I've lost all my innards! Sorry can't write any more—my hand is shaking so much—I can't concentrate, I can't see, I'm sweating—I'm going to be—sick—.

30 July 1942

Feeling much better again—lost some weight and appetite—not allowed to go back to chores yet.

Dad received a letter from Mr Demetriades and wife now in Perth—sent through the Australian Red Cross C/- Japanese Red Cross Society, Tokyo, Japan. How are we going to explain to them that Amber Mansions went under the Japanese bombs. Think Dad wrote to them . . .

Cell 36–A5

Now on the top floor—much brighter and more airy but a struggle coming up and down these flights of steps.

Lady Heath is now in KK Hospital—seriously ill—her baby boy stillborn.

Palled up with Joyce Edwards—we sleep out in E garden every night.

Mosquitos bad sometimes but we have nets over ourselves in a form of a tent and that helps.

We have a library now. Dancing classes in full swing—Barbara Smith teaches tap, ballet and ballroom. Mrs Kronin has the physical training classes.

Had General Elections of the Executive Committee—results—Dr Hopkins re-elected Camp Commandant. Mrs Gregory-Jones, Deputy Camp Commandant. Miss Josephine Foss—Camp Superintendent. Mrs Ferguson—Deputy Camp Superintendent. Diet seems a little better—more rice/water with stewed meat of sorts (maybe a horse or perhaps a cat or a dog?)

4 August 1942

Mrs Gregory-Jones ill and Miss Griffith-Jones elected in her place as Deputy Camp Commandant. Piano recital given by Dr Robinson. Gramophone recital every Monday organised by Mrs Eisinger. Red Cross Corner now in the Lumber Room—doing very well. Camp Credit also started at $5 per head. Shopping allowed once a month.

10 August 1942

Eighteen today—no celebrations—just a quiet day. As a matter of fact nobody knows it's my birthday and I'm not about to spread the news. Feel like a bit of poetry writing so here goes.

Changi Chimes

The first thing you hear
When dawn draws near
A sound that rises and falls
And to sleepy heads calls
To start yet another day
With its chiming lay . . .

13 August 1942   **A Question of Innocence**

Had vaccination for typhoid and cholera.

Had a strange conversation with my stepmother—wanted to know how long since I had my period—Odd! Hadn't thought much about it—in fact, I am glad not to have to wash these horrible, scrappy bits of cloth in buckets of not so soapy water (and you had to be careful that you didn't use too much water!)

Mum—'Have you been sleeping with a man?'

Self—'Don't be silly—you know no man is allowed here without the sentry. Anyway, what do you mean "sleep with a man"?'

She looked hard and long at me, shaking her head—'You no period—too long—see Doc, See Doc today. Now, Now, go, go now' and pushed me towards the dispensary.

Doc—'No! Not you too!' when she saw me.

Confused, I looked at her, not knowing what to say.

Doc—'What is it? Dysentery or malaria?'

Self—'Neither'

Doc—'Then, what can I do for you?'

Self—'Nothing, that I know of except that my stepmother is worried about me not having my period.'

Doc—'How long?'

Self—'I think about four months—haven't worried about it really.'

Doc—'Tell your mother not to worry. A lot of us at the moment are going through the same thing. Nature will right itself eventually and we'll all start cursing the fact that we are females!'

Self—'Then why is my stepmother so upset?'

Doc—'She probably thinks you could be pregnant,' and smiled at me.

Self—'Pregnant? Me? You mean that I'm going to have a baby? Not possible,' shocked, I shook my head—'I haven't been sitting on a man's lap and let him kiss me so I can't have a baby'.

Doc—'Where on earth did you get that idea from, Sheila?'

Self—'Well, in the Convent, I used to hear the older girls whispering about it and saying that if you let a man kiss you, he'll get you pregnant.'

Doc—'I think you and I will have to have a little talk. Come and see me tomorrow afternoon in my cell.'

With that she ushered me out of the door, her arms around my shoulders. Now I'm wondering what the hell she is going to talk about—Have to wait!

14 August 1942
Well, we've had our talk. Talk? It was an education! I did biology at school and know all about eggs being fertilised, etc. but I didn't know it could be so involved—my first sex education—why wasn't I told it in school? What a dumb cluck I am! Talk about the innocence of youth—Gosh! I sure am dumb! And red with embarrassment, as the Doc explained the 'facts of life'!

As I write this I am thinking—with this knowledge am I now a woman or still a child? Do I use this knowledge as a shield to protect my womanhood or childhood? Does this mean that I've crossed the dateline that marks the end of innocence and the beginning of maturing conflicts? Thoughts, feelings, emotions running riot—bah! I'll put them at the back of my mind—I'm not going to get involved with all that in here or ever for that matter—sounds too complicated.

4 September 1942
Lieutenant Okasaki and Tokuda have gone and Asahi has taken their place. He is not as kindly disposed towards us as Okasaki was. I think we could be in for a rough time with him in command.

8 September 1942
George de Broise—one of our boys gave an impromptu concert in E garden—enjoyed by all.

9 September 1942
The Arts and Crafts Exhibition was held in the Red Cross Room—tremendous success. Plenty of exhibits—Mrs Bateman won First Prize for her charming still life of the toy display. Mrs Dawson—1st Prize for landscapes and topographical painting. Miss Tomkins got a special mention in her class and gained a well-deserved first for her delightful cards (Xmas). Miss Renton's dainty handkerchiefs and Xmas cards also won 1st and 2nd respectively. Miss Parfitt with her

outstanding humorous drawing and Mrs Stanley-Cary got a special prize in that class.

The children also had prizes awarded to them in the drawing section . . .

This evening I'm feeling off colour—have a headache and the shivers. I think I'll go to bed early.

10 September 1942

A carefully arranged concert given by the adults under Mrs Milne was held in the Carpenter's Shop.

No more mince—mutton instead. The men gave us another concert in the main courtyard.

Entertainment Committee—Miss Parfitt, Chairman.

For the past two months we have Sikh guards. Had letters from D.N.—not interested in writing back—told him so—now he writes to other girls.

This headache is not going away—I think I'm going to be sick again—taken to hospital.

Malaria!—sweating, shivering—can't get warm! Piles of blankets and hot water bags, still shaking. Temperature up to 104°F! Now hot—now cold. Teeth can't stop chattering—head feels like splitting, can hardly see—exhaustion—stillness—temperature down. Had a change of clothes. Phew! so that's how Malaria gets you—hope not anymore.

1 October 1942

Bathing party to Tanah Mira (about 15 minutes away) enjoyed by all who went. Feeling myself again after malarial attack—taking quinine still—lost weight again! Dr Cecily Williams and Mrs de Mowbray have gone to stay outside doing medical reports.

7 October 1942

Red Cross ship arrived with stores and letters received and allowed to be written— all are censored, of course!

22 October 1942

Day has been hot but this evening there is a cool breeze blowing and we are being entertained by strains of distant music being relayed by the radiogram in the Carpenter's Shop. Mrs Eisinger's carefully thought out concert of classical music—Beethoven featuring the MBC Symphony Orchestra with Heifetz and

便　郵　虜　俘

俘虜收容所
檢閱濟

3
PASSED
BY
CENSOR
328

COMITÉ INTERNATIONAL - CROIX-ROUGE - GENÈVE

Miss Grace B. Allan,

115 Cochrane St., Gardenvale,

Melbourne, Australia.

Changi Internment Camp, Malaya.
    Changi   Nov. 1st 1942

My Dear Sister,
                I trust that you are well & have no
troubles. Sheila & I both sent you cards on the 21st of
June last. We are both sending cards again
this time. Bruce Bridger of Harrietville is
with us. We are all in good health. Tom Hocking
is alive & in good health. As I mentioned previously
poor Bill Warren died of wounds & illness. You
may write to us through the International Red
Cross. Fondest Love from your loving brother Allan
John. C. ALLAN

Toscanini. The few parcels and letters came from South Africa through the Red Cross post—great excitement at getting news from home and friends who left but there were also sad tidings.

Saturday, 24 October 1942

Am in my cell and listening to the music from the men's side. They are playing lighter music. Mrs Eisinger also planned this concert. Oh! Listen to that music—I am carried away from this existence to another world—a beautiful work of music as I wander dreamily through its strains. For just a while, all cares are forgotten. The concert's finished and I am brought to earth again. Short as it was I felt refreshed. Music, music! The very word itself stirs my emotions and makes me forget for a while all weariness and sadness . . .

Sunday, 25 October 1942

Birthday party for Iris Bolton in the E kitchen. Sure we had a long celebration—started a couple of days beforehand with the preparations. There were Mrs Tan, Walton, Thornley-Jordon and Mrs Jennings depipping the dates; grating coconuts and baking lots and lots of cakes and biscuits—they must have saved their supplies for this occasion. Even the children got into the act and created the most beautiful cake of clay with coloured beads and banded with pink paper. It looked so real that some of us were almost tempted to try a piece! There was a large fruit salad placed on the long table beautifully decorated. Lady Thomas made a speech to the birthday girl and Mrs Bolton replied, thanking all who were there to celebrate her birthday—then she led the party to singing songs, old and new. Her daughter, Ivy, was persuaded to dance accompanied by her musical mother to the delight of all present. Dr Hopkins, Miss Foss were also there and the medical and nursing profession were represented by Dr Smallwood, Dr Robinson, Dr Worth, Mrs Doherty and Mrs Farrar. . .

Tuesday, 3 November 1942

It's the Japanese holiday so I'm told and we are allowed to go for a stroll outside the prison walls from 6.30 p.m. to 7.30 p.m. A few of us took the advantage of taking a good look at the outside world for a change. Didn't go far—some just sat and read—others strolled round and through trees. Dr Hopkins led the way—smiling and talking gaily away. My eyes followed her every movement and I wanted to get close to her. When she said goodnight to me, my heart leapt with joy. Oh, I think she's lovely and I like her a lot.

   Yesterday we had the General Meeting held in the Carpenter's Shop at 7 p.m. Dr Hopkins' voice didn't sound too good. She must have a very bad cold. I sure don't envy her her job but she does it well although there is already talk of her being stood down. It's true, you can't please everybody. I think Dr Hopkins is finding that out.

Friday, 6 November 1942   Pow-Wow Circus

Dear diary—do you know where I have been—to the Circus, yes to the Circus! Just imagine it—and it is just over and I have to write it down. It was marvellous, it was wonderful—it was—in fact—everything!—a surprise, a treat and we all enjoyed ourselves.

Before the show started at 7.30 p.m. we were admitted at 7.15 p.m. and imagine our surprise at seeing the 'tallest woman'—half man, half woman—the orang-outang. There was 'the midget' and ambling along 'the fattest woman'. The make-up was perfect but the orang-outang was very well done—it was really something! It took us some time to guess who she was. As the show was about to begin, 3 reporters entered—Dr Worth of the Syonan Slimes, Sister Norah Jones and Mrs Betty Buchnan the Rumour Monger. They were greeted by a shout of laughter as they strode majestically, taking notes and then sat down.

The show started with the 'Lion Act'—the roaring was real enough to frighten the children and obstinacy of one was enough to make one shriek with laughter—Dr Hopkins was nowhere to be seen and I was disappointed until it dawned on me that she may be taking a part in the show.

The second item was 'Czardas'—the tambourine dance—performed by Mrs Jessica St Leon and Billie James. This was followed by 'Mello and Tony' performed by Freddy Bloom and Toby Williams—the stars of the show—at their appearance the building came down with the laughter that shook us and could hardly be suppressed. They made a perfect pair of clowns!

'Stoutheart, the Strongman' (Leonor Palomar) then came into the ring to do his stuff—really strongman feats and we did admire his muscular body. The elephant act came next—the make-up of the elephants was very good and deserved the honours due to them.

No sooner was this over, in came Mrs Bloom with boxing gloves and we were asked by Mrs Palomar if any of us would like to have a boxing match with—when who should appear but Mrs Williams but she only knew how to box with her feet so she brought along 'Hoppy, the Kangaroo' (Dr Hopkins) who hopped and skipped around Mrs Bloom and finally got her down before she realised what was happening.

Interval time—and peanuts were offered around by various people in different costumes. The rest of the items were 'Tishy the Wonder Horse and Mlle Longlong'—it was very clever. 'The Three Hunchbacks' (Jessica St Leon, Billie and Moogie) were a scream.

<u>Wednesday, November 25th, 1942 at 7.30 p.m.</u>

A Changi Mixed Grill SPECIALLY SELECTED FOR THE LADIES AND THE LITTLE ONES.......................................

1. March.   "Under Freedom's Flag (F. Nowowiejaki)
                               The Changi Orchestra.

2. Songs.   Stan. Cottrill.
        " Dance Apache"
3. ~~Stuff & Nonsense~~   ~~"Bones" Kirby.~~ B. Aherne

4. Vocal Selections.   "Go down Moses." (Negro Spiritual)
                       "Lullaby" (D.B.Soul)
                       "On the Lagoons " (Medelssohn)
                       "The Hunters Farewell" (Mendelssohn).
                       "The Huntsmans Chorus. (Weber).
                           The Camp Choir.

5. "With Annie Laurie Round the World".
                     A Musical joke by R.E.
                     ~~Performed by Masters Bolton, De Broise, Jennings, Ricketts, Sharman and Symons.~~
                     Performed by Messrs Chapman, Cottrill, Davidson
                     Eisenger, Farrell, Kauff, Merrifield, Ross and
                     Waters.

6. Singing Lesson.   "Our Gang".
                     Performed by Masters Bolton, De Broise, Jennings,
                     Ricketts, Sharman and Symons.

                     "Popeye"   Mr. Crawshaw.
                     "Donald Duck" Mr. Carter.

7. Suite - "Orientale"   (Popy)
                     1. Les Bayaderes.   2. Reverie.
                     3. Les Almees.   4. Patrouille.
                       The Changi Orchestra.

       Stuff. Nonsence
8. ~~Russian Ballet.~~   ~~Mme. Gurnitzkaya.~~ 'Bones' Kirby.
                     ~~M. Goodrybzki.~~

9. Vocal Selections.   "Stenka Razin."
                     "Evening Bells."
                     "Song of the Volga Boatmen. " Russian Folk Song.
                       The Camp Choir.

                Compere - Noel Rees.

      <u>Orchestra.</u>   <u>Choir.</u>
Violins. Messrs Akrill, Brown,   <u>Tenors.</u> Messrs Bonwick, Chegwin, Cherri-
   Harper Ball, Loveday, Ross   -ngton, Cottrill, Cowgill, Ellis, Haines,
   and Waters.   Hallard, Hilton, Holmes, Hool, Mollison,
Clarinet. Farrel.   Morris, Pash, Peck, Poulain, Price,
Sax.   Harrison.   Shannon, Soul, Syer, Taylor & Thompson.
Trumpet. Cottrill.   Basses. Anderson, Baughman, Carter,
Piano.   ~~Eisenger.~~   Cassels, Coney, Coulson, Dant, Davidson
Accord's. Merrifield & Candiliotis. Duff, Garcia, Geeke, Grove-White, Harrison,
Bass.   Kauff.   Hockenhull, Hodge, De Jager, Llewellyn
Drums.   Chapman.   Murray, Osborne, Pendlebury, Smith, Spr
                              Spragg, Thamsen, Thomas, Thomson, Waters
                              and Wright.

      Conductor. W.Crofts.   Conductor. C.Van Hien.

'The Tightrope Artists' (Mrs Kent and Sue Williams) took our breath away when they did their 'balancing' act.

'The Fairy Queen' I think stole the show—it was performed by Mrs Isabel Bentley who was dainty as any fairy queen could be who suffers from rheumatics!

'The Seal Act' (Mrs Henderson) made us think of days gone by—the imitation was flawless.

The last but not the least act was our own clowns—'The Honey Bee Act'—after which the show ended with 'God Save Our King'. What a wonderful night—I had my first real laugh since the war started. Well done! Well done, everybody. I'm sure we'll all go to sleep dreaming of being at the Circus again—maybe this time we'll be out of this 'Hell-hole'!

Wednesday, 25 November 1942   **The Men's Concert**
We were allowed to see the men's concert—permission given by Nakajima and Mr Chuchitana. The concert was held in the courtyard with sentries keeping an eye on proceedings! Took our places in the main courtyard at 7.15 p.m.

Stage looked great though somewhat small. The actors were all out in the yard (other prisoners were behind the grills—saw Dad and waved to him). At 7.45 p.m. the show started with a march 'Under Freedom's Flag'. Sat on some stone tiles which rocked perilously to and fro as I kept time to the music . . .

The Camp Orchestra was well and truly appreciated by all. The last on the programme was the Camp Choir and we marvel at those wonderful voices and we all sang 'God Save Our King'—after which Dr Hopkins called out for 'Three cheers for our men'—we cheered as loudly as our lungs and voices would allow! It was a lovely evening and we do appreciate what the men have done for us. Hope there'll be another before long—God bless the men.

There is an outbreak of diphtheria and isolation of patients in progress. George de Broise is going over to the Men's Camp. Relatives other than husbands and wives are allowed to meet every Thursday for 15 minutes, they'll be busy exchanging messages for husbands and wives!

Friday, 27 November 1942   **Bathing Party**
Allowed out today—left at 2 p.m. saw Dad as we went through the main courtyard—waved to him. Taken to a new spot further up—it was rather a long walk and a hot one. Passed some of our soldiers working in the sun—they looked really thin and so brown. Walked beside Miss Griffith-Jones and talked all the way—it certainly made the walk more enjoyable. When we arrived at the place I was taken up with the lovely view—all that sand and the cool, clean water rushing

on the shore. There was not a trace of cloud in the clear blue sky. The air smelt fresh and you could feel that salt spray stinging.

There are two houses here—empty—and a third occupied by the Japs. Went down a series of steps to the beach—could hardly wait to get in the water. Together with Mrs Raybach we swam out—it was beautiful as we dived under the waves and let that lovely cool water relax our weary bodies.

Played with the children later on the beach and even had them standing on my shoulders so they could dive into the water. It was great fun and I was filled with exquisite joy of being alive! Alas, too soon it was over and we had to get ourselves back to that concrete building where once more we will be viewing the outside world behind bars!

Monday, 30 November 1942   St Andrew's Day Celebrations

Tonight at eight we went into the Carpenter's Shop to watch and join the Caledonians celebrating St Andrew's Day.

Miss Valerie Burgin played the piano and we joined in singing the Scottish song. Mrs Millard sang 'Annie Laurie' which was much appreciated. There were dances too led by Mrs Elizabeth Ennis. It was fun watching Dr Hopkins and Dr Worth trying some of the dance steps. I watched Dr Hopkins and thought how tired and thin she is looking. After Miss Burgin, Mrs Hope took her turn on the piano.

We joined hands as we sang 'Auld Lang Syne'. It was most enjoyable.

Dear Diary—isn't Dr Hopkins just 'something'—she's so different to the others or am I biased?

9 December 1942

Mrs Ong is leaving us today to join her husband—we do congratulate her on her release. And talking about releases—I've just been released from the hospital bed with another bout of Malaria—it came on so suddenly after St Andrew's Day celebrations—still a bit weak on my 'pins' but well enough to do my chores!

10 December 1942   Piano recital by Dr Robinson

The Military relations have elected a Committee composed of Bloom, Kent, Cornelius, Mulvany and Noble, to see what steps can be taken to impress the Japanese authorities the urgent need for initiation of communication between military husbands, wives and other relatives.

It is just over a year since war broke out in Malaya. It has been a full year in more ways than one can imagine—most of it not very pleasant—in fact, in some instances, downright frightening. Hope 1943 will bring peace and perhaps release from these confounded walls!

Both Mrs White and Mrs Aiken are sick—have been working with them since Mrs Macarthy became our floor walker in October.

11 December 1942

Mr Asahi is now back—he has been to Sumatra where he visited several internment camps. It is understood that he has brought back a list of the internees in Palembang Camp and the list will be given to us, and complete lists of all internees in Sumatra will also be handed to us—When??

Sunday, 12 December 1942

Two new internees arrived today—Mrs Deakes and her son, Paddy. They arrived from the Andaman Islands and they certainly looked very tired and badly in need of a rest after an exhausting journey in very bad weather.

The weekly meetings between relatives are back on the agenda now that our Camp is out of quarantine for diphtheria.

Monday, 13 December 1942

We said goodbye to Christine Clark who is going to live at the Convent of the Sacred Heart. It's a sad parting for Mrs Clark and her husband who is in the Men's Camp.

Wednesday, 15 December 1942

Mrs Noble has been asking for some months to be allowed to have her son, Bobby, with her and today she got her wish when Bobby arrived in Camp to be reunited with his mother in time for Christmas. The Red Cross Coffee Party was a huge success. There was food of all kinds to tempt us. The toy collection would thrill the hearts of those between one year and ninety!!!

Mrs Dixon worked long and hard to make patchwork jackets and quilts.

Dolly Toby created a perfect little Malay hut which brought forth a lot of ohs and ahs! There were dolls of all descriptions. Father Christmas will not be out of a job this year.

16 December 1942

Mr Asahi announced that his Xmas present to the Camp is full permission to everyone to meet between the hours of 10 a.m. and 12 noon on Christmas Day.

The list of names of women and children interned in Palembang is up in the Carpenter's Shop. Mr Asahi who brought us the list from Sumatra said he had visited about twenty internment camps. Promised to let us have the full list of internees in Sumatra as soon as he received them. Also said that of all the camps he visited, Changi is the best! Gosh! Hate to think what the other camps are like.

Eight hundred and fifty Red Cross letters arrived last week—most of them were from England and South Africa. Not many for the Women's Camp but no doubt some of us will receive news in their husbands' letters.

Since being here we've been lucky to be allowed to have Church Services on Sundays. Father Cosgrave is one of the Roman Catholic Priests.

20 December 1942

Feeling very tired—recovered from an attack of malaria—*again*—this time ended up with a chest infection. The sisters tell me I have two *beautiful* red roses on my cheeks! I can't be bothered to do anything—all I want to do is sleep but I must continue to write things down before I forget. Dear Diary, I am really too tired today but I must, I must go on. All of a sudden there is pandemonium—we have a visit from the Jap captain. I mustn't let him see my book—what to do?— sat on it while he did his rounds—looked at me—must have thought I was too sick to care about anything much. Phew! What a relief when he left the ward.

22 December 1942

Still in hospital, cough still troublesome and painful. Heard Dr Hopkins is sick and is also in hospital. What is it about her that makes me want to be with her? I look through my book of poetry and come across 'Rosaline' by T. Lodge . . .

Vague fancies and strange longings fill my being and when I go to sleep I find myself repeating the strange, haunting lines penned by Edgar Alan Poe—about his wife he loved and lost . . .

> For the moon never beams without bringing me dreams
> Of the beautiful Annabel Lee;
> And the stars never rise, but I feel the bright eyes
> Of the beautiful Annabel Lee.

How beautiful those words—how sad—how hopeless it was. And then I think of Dr Hopkins and hope she'll get better soon . . . Does this mean that I have a 'crush' on the good doctor—I sure have—I think she's just wonderful!

23 December 1942   **Nativity Play**

Written by Mrs Loveridge was performed in the Carpenter's Shop. This was produced by Mrs Nelson. Miss Muriel Clark was in charge of the costumes. Mrs Symons and Mary Scott helped with the 'Curtain'. Credit goes to Mrs K Mackenzie for the make-up. With assistants Dolly Toby and Edna Aldworth, Miss Rackman took charge of the scenery. Miss Margaret Young gave the pianoforte solo—'Jesus joy of man's desiring' by Bach. She also played all the accompaniments.

Mrs Millard gave voice to 'The Magnificat' and 'Sleep Holy Babe' delightfully sung by Mrs Hilda Barbour. They were accompanied by the Humming Birds Choir.

The Sunday School children had a part in the play which tells the story of Christmas and the real meaning of Christmas . . . The angels' wings made up the 'Curtain' and it was fantastic. I have been busy making a tablecloth (see sketch opposite) to give as a present to Dr Hopkins. I have finished it and it was sent to the Men's Exhibition. It took me two months to finish it—off and on between bouts of malaria.

24 December 1942

Our collection of Christmas toys is increasing so does our admiration at the ingenuity and talents of the creators. We had the relatives' meeting as usual. Tonight Christmas carols from 8 p.m. to 9 p.m. Everyone is busy doing something towards Christmas. The Carpenter's Shop is a hive of activity—Christmas tree being decorated and bits and pieces of decorations scattered all over the place. Guess, eventually it will all take shape and the stage set in time for Santa's arrival.

Friday, 25 December 1942   **Christmas Day**

Our first Christmas in captivity! Went to bed early last night and listened to carols by the Men's choir. Later last night got up and helped with delivering the presents to the children.

This morning up early and attended the Xmas service. The doors were opened between 10 a.m.–12 noon between the two camps. Lots of people milling around. Saw Dad and we both had tears in our eyes—together with Mum we went over to the Men's Camp and had a look around. Saw Mr Marriot and thanked him for our presents. Talked and talked about how we are coping and what we'll do when we get out of here.

When the gong sounded, it was time for us to leave. The two hours flew into nothingness, wished it had been longer. Dad is looking thin and I don't think he is very well.

Children's Christmas Tree 7.15 p.m.

Went to the Carpenter's Shop where the children, mothers and others were together round the Christmas tree. There were toys and more toys on the stage behind it. The toys, we were told, were done by the men and the soldiers—they did look wonderful—the men who make them are really clever and must have taken a great deal of trouble to find the materials—there were trains, little cars, houses, animals of all kinds—in fact, too many to mention.

Lady Thomas was the hostess—Mrs Milne read out the names and handed the parcels to Santa Claus (Mrs Kennard). The boys that were from the Men's Camp came too to get their presents.

At a certain sign from Mrs Gregory, I pushed the trolley with Santa Claus sitting on a chair. *He* was greeted with shouts of laughter and handed the presents to the children.

It was a happy gathering and we gave three cheers for Lady Thomas and another rousing three cheers for Santa Claus.

After, Mrs Eisinger got the radiogram going for anyone who wanted to dance. Dr Hopkins came over to thank me for her present—said showed the tablecloth to her husband and he liked it very much.

It is very late and I am ready for sleep but dear Diary, I must write all this down before I forget the details of our first Christmas in Changi Prison!

Saturday, 26 December 1942   **Bathing Party and Fancy Dress Ball**

Mum was sick last night so I undertook to do her chores. Got up early and went for a shower—Holy of holies! no hot water! so got dressed and did the chores, then did the pots and helped with the breakfast. At nine went to do my own chores—cleaning drains. In fact the whole morning was taken up with helping others get on with their work—seems as if we've had a night out and too tired to carry on with our chores!

At a quarter to two we went off for our bathing party. Saw the POWs working in the fields as we went by—they gave us a wave and a whistle!

Got in the rain and did it pour but that didn't worry us—we'd get wet anyway going for our swim. It was lovely but how I wished we were free and not have to go back to our cells.

This evening was our Fancy Dress Ball held in the Carpenter's Shop. Marvellous all the get together and the different costumes—there was Mrs Ennis dressed as the 'Queen of Hearts', Mrs Bentley won first prize for being original—she was dressed as the 'Departed Spirits'. Mrs Kinnear had leaves all over her, labelled 'What Changi will wear in 1943'. Mrs Lancaster looked really 'Indian' in her dress. Mary Winters looked cute as a 'Chinese'. Dolly Toby and Mrs Eisinger came as a 'Mysterious Person'. Prize for the prettiest went to Xenia who came as a 'Hawaiian Girl'. Kera Clarke was the 'Pirate Bold'. Mrs Macindo in sarong Kabaya was a 'Javanese'.

To top it all—the prize for the best went to Mrs Bach for her creation of 'The Rat in Alice in Wonderland'.

Everybody enjoyed themselves—for the time being we forgot about being in here. We joked and laughed and marvelled at the wonderful ways we have been able to provide for this evening's entertainment. Three cheers for Mrs Smith, our organiser—'Hip, hip, pip etc'.

Another tiring day and so to sleep!

31 December 1942   **A fairy play of Sleeping Beauty**
Arranged by Mrs Cutler and Mrs Dickson for the children (adults included!) We certainly have a talented lot of people in our midst—fantastic costumes and marvellous acting. The play was most enjoyable and greatly appreciated by all present. I really don't know where they get all the ideas—the Entertainment Committee deserves our thanks.

1943

1 January 1943   **'Happy New Year'**

Rang loud and clear this morning—sez who?—we all did and hope that it will be a better year. However, chores have to be done—Mrs Mitchell and I cleared the grids and then helped Mrs Bach to clear all the greenery.

We had our usual relatives' meeting—saw Dad and had a serious conversation—spoke about the future and if I had any idea what I wanted to do—write, of course, but Dad shook his head and advised me to have a talk with Dr Hopkins or Miss Foss. I don't know what I want to do and who knows what the future has in store for me or any of us here—heaven only knows how long the war is going to last or even if we will live through all this.

This evening saw the noticeboard with news that four of the Executive Officers of the Committee are resigning. Oh dear! Here we go again—Camp politics!

4 January 1943   **General Meeting: Politics and More Politics!**

From the very beginning I've steered clear of Camp politics but today's 'General Meeting' is, I think, the most outstanding of all the 'General and Extraordinary Meetings' that has been held from the time we came here.

There is always a lot of arguments and back-stabbings going on at these meetings. Today was no exception—in fact, it was one long argument—it went on and on and round and round and they got no further than from where they started.

It went on for more than two hours and the meeting had to be adjourned and continued tomorrow.

There was such a lot of accusations and whatnot, that I could hardly remember Dr Hopkins' report but as I consider this to be a very important meeting being the end of the present Committee I feel that I must get a copy of the minutes . . .

Changi School—Our School

Started in a garage at Katong Camp on 24th February, 1942—the suggestion came from Dr Elliot to Mrs B. Lumsden Milne—not so much school but something for the children to do and not be at a loose end. The idea of school on top of our discomforts such as spending a couple of days scraping grease and dirt off the floor and then scrubbing it wasn't the flavour of the month!

However, things began to happen—we balanced planks on low crates for seats and the higher crates made reasonable tables. Mrs Eisinger, Miss Griffith-Jones, Mrs Stanley-Cary and Miss Moore were willing helpers. Slowly it took shape— pencils, paper, chalks and textbooks began to appear. The hours were irregular, like our meal times but we had a school of sorts!

Coming to Changi Prison helped to improve our school condition. More books, exercise books, pencils, etc. arrived from the outside world and Christmas brought us a lot more. We get daily religious instruction from Miss Rank, Mrs Nelson, Miss Robinson and Miss Russel-Davis. The rest of the teaching staff included Miss Parfitt, Mrs Blackman, Miss Renton, Miss Summers, Miss von Hagt and Mrs White and there are also others on a temporary basis.

8 January 1943

Results of General Meeting—Dr Hopkins re-elected as Camp Commandant; Mrs Nixon—Deputy Camp Commandant; Mrs Ferguson—Camp Superintendent; Mrs Jennings—Deputy Camp Superintendent. There is going to be a Literary Competition, open to members of our Camp, arranged by the Men's Leisure Hour Committee—I think I'll try to put in an entry—a short story, perhaps!

9 January 1943

Concert presented by the Women's Section, shown to the men in the main courtyard.

13 January 1943   Account from the Weekly Pow-Wow (page 5)

Of course the topic of the past week was the concert we were allowed to give the men. Joy of Joys! What an audience it was! The dream of every performer's life. 'S funny when you see the men, one by one, coming over on fatigues they don't seem too irresistible. In fact, some aren't at all attractive. But see them all in a mass, freshly shaved and polished and bearing the brrr of their grand deep voices, a feeling of great love and proud possessiveness comes over one . . . 'These are our men.'

The eyes of the women sparkled, their voices rang out loud and clear (and not much off key). Oh, they look good. Considering ten months in Changi, they looked superlative.

We are not going to give an account of the concert. The acts were taken from past entertainments which we all saw and the dress rehearsal on Friday showed what had been chosen to go over. It was an excellent choice though a number of items

1. THE CHOIR   Conductor: Betty Milne

2. DUTCH DANCE
   Mesdames d'Almeida, Allen, Criblens, Edwards,
   Greenway, E., M. and R. Von Hagt, James,
   Palomar.

3. INTERNATIONAL INTERLUDE
   Mesdames A. Williams, Eisinger, Stanley-Carey,
   Reyersbach, Clark, Coalen, Hodgson

4. Billie James   TAP DANCE

5. Xenia Billiewicz, Soprano.

6. Mary Winters   "PAN"

7. Mike Kent   A SPOT OF MIKENTERY

8. Barbara Smith   POLISH DANCE

9. THE CHOIR

10. Angela Kronin   INDIAN DANCE

11. Iris Parfitt   "AT THE CINEMA"

12. HARLEQUIN AND COLUMBINE
    Billie James and Mary Winters

13. Betty Millard, Mezzo.

14. Constance Medwyn   "MRS 'ARRIS"

15. APACHE DANCE   Angela Kronin and Mike Kent

16. Hilda Barbour, Soprano.

17. Joanna Criblens   "GROUSING AS USUAL"

18. A CAFE IN SPAIN
    Barbara Smith, Leonor Palomar, Maureen
    Eisinger.

19. Mary Winters   CHINESE FAN DANCE

20. BALLET DU DONJON
    Prima Ballerina: Iris Parfitt.
    Corpses de Ballet: Mlles. Auger, Bryant, Flet-
    cher, Grant, Jeffries, E. Jones, Scott, Williams.

##########

CHOIR: Mesdames A. M. Allen, L. Allen, Cuthbe, Early, Eisinger,
Fletcher, Grant, Jeffries, Kinnear, Kirkbride, Lopez, Mackenzie,
Mather, Renton, Robinson, Scott, Smith, Sparks, Stanley-Carey, Van
Roode, Von Hagt, West.

ACCOMPANISTS: Valerie Buroin, Hilda Barbour, R. L. Eber,
Pauline Dickinson, Margaret Hope.

SCREEN: Mmes. Jeltes, La Clocia, Sullivan, Thomas, White, M.
Williams.

CHOREOGRAPHY: Items 2, 4, 8, 12, 18 arranged by Barbara
Smith. Items 10 and 19 arranged by Angela Kronin.

DECOR: Ann Courtenay.

MAKE-UP: Rona Cutler.

Programme for the concert presented by the Women's Section, 9 January 1943.

had to be left out . . . probably to go over in the next concert, if permission for another is granted. Here, however, are some flashes from Saturday night.

Angela Kronin's beautiful hands in the Indian Dance. (It is good to see Mrs Kronin looking so well again after her long spell of being off colour. We hear that she will soon resume her dancing classes . . . welcome news for the camp.)

So Betty Milne speaks Tamil! 'We're not surprised. She does so many things well, what's a bit of Tamil more or less?'

The precision and ease of Joyce Edwards and Sheila Allan as one couple of the highly successful Dutch Dance. (Those rehearsals in the corridor were not wasted.)

Watching Mrs Greenway in both the Dutch Dance and the International number it was impossible to believe that she had a grown-up son sitting in the audience.

We knew Marion Reyerabach was Hungarian and had that certain Hungarian spirit, but we never suspected she would be able to put it across the footlights with quite so much zip.

Didn't that steely blue-grey dinner frock suit Mrs Lucian Allen perfectly? One look at Mr Lucian Allen gave the answer. We suspect it was not the frock alone.

Mrs Barbour's fine stage presence, in spite of the difficulties . . . giggling children during dress rehearsal, and unending chiming clocks during the performance itself. She carried it off jolly well.

The entire audience thrilled to Xenia Billiewizc's voice . . . we have never heard her sing so beautifully. Mrs Murray Ainsley must have been very proud.

The electrician himself was most annoyed that there was no direct centre lighting. All the more credit to Iris Parfitt for the brilliance of her monologue. A great deal of the success of the show was due to her untiring hard work . . . and of course her knowledge and talent.

The lighting too kept Mary Winter's Fan Dance from having its best effect. Incidentally we were under the impression that Pauline Dickinson had arranged that dance. It seemed to have her touch. Perhaps we were wrong.

Lest the criticism of the lighting be misinterpreted it must be said right away that the stage, its decor and the lighting were terrific considering the time and material available.

Oh, apropos Mrs Dickinson, in the last week's write-up of the pantomime we left out all mention of the masked 'Gym' class. Now every time we pass along AIV the masks stick out their tongues at us. They graced (or disgraced?) Barbara Smith, Sheila Allan, Isabella Bentley, Poppy Rackman and Helen Kirkbride.

These masks were made by John Eber and painted by Mr Walker. And now, we hope, they'll stop making faces (the masks not Messrs Eber and Walker).

There is always something a shade fishy about one woman saying another looked beautiful but what did you think of Mesdames La Cloche, Sullivan, Jean White and Mesdemoiselles Jeltes, Thomas and Marian Williams as the 'Glamour Curtains'? (Have you heard Gene Bales' crack that in the race to be in the show F. Bloom won by a nose. Ain't it 'ell?)

Speaking of glamour, imagine anyone looking like Kyra Clark and being nervous about going on stage. Yet she was . . . though the audience would never have thought it.

Sorry we could not see Robert Eisinger's face when Maureen appeared as a Spanish Waiter . . . masterly change from the chic chanteuse of the International number.

Sometimes little things are so beautifully non-Changi-makeship they do the heart good, e.g. Kathleen Mackenzie's perfect match in frock and lipstick.

We must tear ourselves away from last Saturday. One way out is to thank here and now, the women who have made Pow-Wow possible.

First and foremost Toby Williams has nobly done all the hardest work right from the very first edition. Pow-Wow is much like an Amah Baby brought into the world by a mother who adores it but who leaves the practical part of its development, that is all the nasty chores to someone else. This child owes its welfare mainly to 'Amah' Williams.

Thanks too, to Constance Sleep who typed for many months and whose work was taken over by Eve McCarthy. Since the star charts started Ailsa West has been spending hours laboriously copying them . . . really tiresome work. Ena Hunt, until her illness spent much time and thought on the weekly Puzzle Page . . . with Judy Good's help. And thank you to our chief contributors: Mary Thomas, Mrs Taplyn, Helen Beck, Dorothy Andrew, Mrs Rattray, never forgetting the illustrations of Iris Parfitt and Joan Stanley-Cary.

With reference to a letter received today . . . will all readers please realise that though writers have likes and dislikes, Pow-Wow as a paper has only the former. If Pow-Wow says anything pleasant about one person it is never a left-handed crack at another. If we omit some obvious tribute it is due not to malice after thought but to natural mental limitations plus a vitamin deficiency.

We do not know what sort of welcome our latest internees, Mrs Deakes and Mrs Younge received upon their arrival. Apart from political [affairs] this Camp is not very demonstrative but by now these newcomers must have felt that if these conditions are any better than the one they left we are jolly glad to have them here. If they disliked coming we commiserate. One never gets to like Changi but one does get more used to it.

Great excitement in the Rose Garden on Monday when Winkie Kirwan returned after his long spell in hospital. His mother, her eyes shining with a can-it-be-true-he's-back expression could hardly get near him. Winkie has a new engine . . . and the other lads had spotted it.

Changi hospitality really needs recording. Whenever did we have such parties as, for instance, Norah Jones' elevenses on Saturday? Coffee rich with santan [milk expressed from grated coconut] and sweetened with gula malacca.

And a supper cake mixed by Norah and Molly Hill (Norah gave the recipe and it seemed to consist of all the food rations except soup and sardines for the last fortnight) and baked by 'Bully'. Seen behind big pieces of cake were Ena Hunt, Betty Burnham (crumb gobbling), Joan Boston and Eve MacCarthy.
Editor F. Bloom AIV30.

11 January 1943

Dr Hopkins went to Miyako this morning for a rest and will not be back for a week or so.

Dear 'Dream Mother'—I am thinking of you and wishing you well. You look so worn-out and I know you worry about us. Rest, rest as much as you can and come back to us ready to do battle for us with the Japs. I hear we are going to get another 250 more internees so you'll have a big job ahead of you—may you overcome all the difficulties and obstacles that may arise.

15 January 1943

Dr Hopkins returned from the Miyako Hospital and is now resting in the Sanatorium. Still looking terribly thin.

19 January 1943

Dr Cicely Williams gave an informal talk about her experiences in Singapore during the past four months. The unusual life led by her and Mrs Katherine de Boubray out on parole in enemy occupied territory was most vividly and humorously described by Dr Williams, who had long ago endeared herself to the Camp as doctor, speaker and woman.

Snippets of odds and ends! . . . We have in our midst a very cheeky sparrow named Herbert. Poor bird was saved from drowning in one of our drains. Eunice Austen-Hofer nursed and trained him—he is so tame that he's forgotten his lowly origin and struts, flutters and cheeps his way around us. His manners are appalling—just ask Nancy Gregory what he thought of Shaw's play! As to trying to get into the bridge game—the cards are not safe with him around.

Hurricane Alley is well named—so poor Miss Webster found out—she left her tray with her real china bowls and cups unprotected from the wind!

23 January 1943

The bathing Picnic took place today and was enjoyed by all who went. Fine weather and tide was in. These excursions away from Changi Prison are a real treat. I didn't go in for a swim—feel a cold or something coming—not malaria again!

25 January 1943

Dr Hopkins went back to Miyako. I'm back in Hospital—it's malaria again! Rumours of new internees and preparations of how to receive them and where to accommodate them are being discussed by the Housing Committee. Mrs Mulvany had a hut erected for the use of night sisters as sleeping quarters during the day and for those who want some quiet. Mass is celebrated there every Sunday.

1 February 1943

Dr Hopkins expected back—Mrs Woods asked if I'd mind doing M's [Dr Hopkins'] washing. Would I mind—what a question!

Permission granted for weekly lectures by the men—it will be a very welcome addition to our entertainment programme.

Mr Adrian Clark was our first lecturer and entertained us this evening with many amusing personal reminiscences of the Law!

Poor Herbert—he has gone, I'm told, where little birdies go when they become tasty morsels for Simba, the cat! That's life!

4 February 1943   Reflection Time!

Ever since we first landed in internment we've thought that things have to get worse before they start to get better. Have we accepted that fact?—I would say so as we seem to make the best of things—especially the children—there's the schoolroom where we can learn and study (that does while away part of the time!) There's the Rose Garden where we play and spend time entertaining in the Carpenter's Shop. The older boys lend a hand in helping too. The older girls (that means me too) look after the very young. Somehow we manage to keep up a high standard of health, conduct, education and some measure of happiness.

With poor food, hardly space to move, nature and beauty are sadly missed and the worse part of it all there is no home life—that family life which is the birthright of all. Despite that we are managing to survive and grow into as fine a group as can be found anywhere.

Looking around me I see all this is possible through the sacrifice, hard work and cooperation of every woman here. There are mothers who worry about us. The doctors and nurses look after our health. The teachers take care of our mental development and the entertainment committee gives us the humour to cope with our depression. Praise goes also to all the sweepers, drain workers who work tirelessly to keep the camp clean—not forgetting our Kitchen Squad who manages to feed us best as they could with what they are given—we, the children, are their responsibility and it's a responsibility they take seriously. How wonderful they are and I hope that I will never forget them when we leave here—end of my musing!

6 February 1943

Nip came round last night on AV. Something happened and Dr Smallwood was slapped for interfering. Miss Foss spoke quietly to him in Malay—'a quiet answer turneth wrath away' as he calmed down and went away. Dr Smallwood was furious indeed.

8 February 1943

M returned today. The Nip came around again for the last two nights. Last night Mr Johns accompanied him on his rounds. Our lecture nights are becoming popular. Tonight we visited Tunis via Mr McInery's delightful lecture—we could almost taste the delicacies of the country, he described and what would we have given to have our teeth sink into those luscious fruits he managed to bring into our minds' vision by his eloquence!

11 February 1943   Classical Concert

This is our first classical concert given by the men. It was to be in the courtyard but because of the rain it was held in the Printers' Shop. And what a concert—I enjoyed it so much that I had tears running down my cheeks . . .

It was a lovely two hours of enjoyment and pleasure indescribable.

Music, music and more music as tonight is something I crave.

13 February 1943

Dr Williams gave us our first lecture on First Aid in the schoolroom . . .

This morning the Red Cross Hut in the Rose Garden was officially opened—we had a coffee party—50 of us present, we all contributed in some way to make this Hut attractive and comfortable as it's going to be a place of quiet retreat where we can escape to read and relax whatever!

Mrs Mulvany made it possible with the arrangements for the building of the Hut—there were plenty of helpers including the men who built the Hut and guess what—it only cost $8.50 in actual cash! It is a good place to get away from all the noise and congested space around us.

Friday, 19 February 1943

An unexpected treat—light orchestral concert by the men in the Rose Garden for an hour—it was very welcomed and hope we will be permitted for it to be a regular event. We are now allowed to go out for walks on Sundays, Wednesdays and Saturdays from 6 p.m.–8 p.m.

Saturday, 20 February 1943
Election held for Camp Commandant—candidates: Dr Cicely and Mrs Nixon—
results—Dr C. Williams Commandant—172 votes and Mrs Nixon—158 votes and
has consented to continue as deputy. Mrs Gregory resigned as secretary and Mrs
Brooks has taken her place.

Dear Diary—is it a year since we surrendered? and what a year it has been! I
couldn't think of a worse year in my life or for that matter in most of the people's
lives in this place—most of us I am sure have feelings of gloom and being 'down
in the dumps' from time to time. The thought of not knowing what's going to
happen and how long we are going to be inside this rotten place makes me feel
both angry and glum—to think that I thought (we all thought) we are going to
be interned for a few months and twelve months later we are still here—a little
worse for wear—mentally I think I'm coping reasonably—physically, I'm not too
sure—I'm losing a lot of weight and the dysentery and malaria does get me down
a bit but I'm still on my feet and I'm sure I haven't gone mad since coming here!

However long it takes I must make sure that I don't lose my sense of humour
and try to live each day with tolerance—look to the future with hope because
there has got to be a 'future' when all this will end and we can begin to live
like normal human beings again.

And now I think of Dr Hopkins—my Dream Mother [later called M] and I
think of her every day and night and she appears before me, not like a memory
but as a vision. It isn't that beauty of face and form that dazzles one at the sight
of a beautiful being and then fades away as suddenly as a blossom in bloom.
It's the harmony of her whole being—the reality of every emotion—the spirituality
of expression—the perfect union of her body and soul. True beauty is sweetness
and sweetness is the spiritualising of the gross, the corporeal and the earthly.
It is the spiritual presence which transforms ugliness into beauty. The more I
look upon this vision of her before me, the more I perceive, above all else, the
magnetic beauty of her person. Oh! what happiness is near me! But is this all—to
be shown the summit of earthly bliss, then be thrust out into the flat, sandy wastes
of existence? To love and then be forever alone! Once to believe and then forever
to doubt! Once to see the light and then forever to be blinded! Will all this happen
to me?

'Poor fool!' I sometimes think, 'Poor fool!' Grow up girl, grow up! She doesn't
know you exist—I mean nothing to her. Think, think—how the moon sheds its
light upon the dark dull water of the river and reflects itself clearly in the smallest
drops—in like manner, she shines upon this dark life and I feel her gentle radiance
reflected in my heart—but dare I hope for a warmer glow?

Enough of my ramblings—I must be going 'nuts'!

The tablecloth pattern I embroidered as a present for Dr Elinor Hopkins.

Miss Josephine Foss, the camp super-intendent who carried notes and messages between the Men's and Women's Camps. (Original print)

Taken in 1946 at my aunt's place in Gardenvale, Victoria, shortly after my arrival in Australia.

'A' Flight, 273 Fighter Squadron, Singapore, 20 September 1945. 'Jinx' Jordan marked with an 'X'.

Monday, 22 February 1943

Mr Osbourne-Jones came over and gave a very entertaining lecture on the subject of English Wit and Humour.

Supper now at 5.15 p.m. because of our walks outside.

Tuesday, 23 February 1943

Had our bathing party—usual place—I do look forward to this outing—I love swimming and it makes me feel so-oo good afterwards. We often see our soldiers on our way there and back—they seem to be doing a lot of digging—never miss giving us a wave. Some of them look awfully thin and sunburnt.

Friday, 26 February 1943

Arts and Crafts Exhibition held in the Printer's Shop at 11 a.m.—the men—Bennett, Harrison and Walker were the judges but the women will judge needlework and cooking sections—a successful venture for all concerned.

Yesterday we had our usual relatives meeting. Saw Dad—he is not looking very well—has Beri-Beri I think.

Later today we had a practice session for our Dancing Exhibition arranged by Mrs Barbara Smith. There was also a 'Bridge Drive'—prizes won by Dr Hopkins, Mrs Elkins and Mrs Garcia.

By order of the Jap—our evening shower will be between 8.45 p.m. to 9.30 p.m. in the future. This cut in time is to help conserve water. We are asked to conserve water and electricity because the supply of both to the Camp depends on electrically driven engines. The load on the engines is in great excess of that for which they were designed and the aim is to avoid wearing out of irreplaceable parts!

Monday, 1 March 1943

Not too slowly but very surely Mr Spotwood won the interest and hearts of the audience this evening with his lecture on 'Life in a German Prison Camp, 1918'. I hope that in twenty-five years (though not interned again!) please!!! I'll be able to make Changi so entertaining. Miss Poppy Tackham is retiring from her post of head gardener—thanks to her—she has done much to improve the original Changi as any others in here with the help of her assistants. Judy Good is taking over. We still have to conform to blackout regulations and when you can't sleep and no lights to read by it sure makes you feel like kicking someone just to create a diversion!

Thursday, 4 March 1943

Relatives' meeting as usual. General Meeting 7.30 p.m. . . . Dr Williams' first report—everything went fairly smoothly but there was still some strain of enmity in the atmosphere. Earlier during the day—reports of several women having an argument and almost coming to blows—wonder what that's all about and who were the women? Sheila! stop being a nosy-parker!

Monday, 8 March 1943

Mr Shellbeare's charming and instructive lecture this evening left us with the sincere hope that he would be allowed to return and finish his account of Mt Everest. Now the First Aid Classes are taken over by Dr Hopkins.

Friday, 12 March 1943

The first time a women was tried, convicted and sentenced in Changi!—confined in a cell on AIV for 15 days. It is very sad and unfortunate but I guess we must also learn to be forgiving and once the law is satisfied we must also be satisfied and not further persecute the woman after she has served her sentence. Unfortunately there are some uncharitable females in here and in Changi there is no escape from malicious tongues!

Friday, 26 March 1943

Since my last entry I've had another malarial attack and spent the first couple of days on the floor in the hospital—wasn't a very bad one this time and got over it pretty quickly—had to because of the rehearsals for our dancing display—'the show must go on' and all that jazz!

Missed out on 'Why read Shakespeare?' by Reverend Colin King. I think I would have enjoyed it.

We now have three Sisters of the Poor interned. Fancy putting the nuns in here!

Heard through the grapevine about the last visit of the Jap—'He came in about 10 the other night, Fergie and I (Mrs Jennings) quickly got out of bed and accompanied him—went to AIII and were "shushed" but when they found it was a Nip on his rounds, they giggled. He then decided to try AIV—Dr Williams joined us. There were so many beds along the passage that he gave up halfway and came down. On the top of the stairs Mrs Nixon joined us—he must have felt annoyed and wondered how many more women were going to join up and escort him. He came to E Block and nearly slipped down the steps. He left us after this but oh! it was funny.'

Friday, 2 April 1943   **Fair Day**

Had been busy getting ready for today. It was a good fine morning. Went to bed early last night and up early—tea was already made. There was a long queue waiting for the bath both in E and A Blocks. By half past three most of us were ready. I had the Nasi Goreng Stall with the Edwards near A Kitchen.

The men who were helping the stall came in first and we started serving. At four, the others simply poured in—the relatives went straight up to the 'Floors' but they were soon turned out by the Japs and Sikhs who came and mingled amongst us. Saw Mr Gleenie, Bridger, Sanderson and many old friends. The stalls did a roaring trade. Dad came over with my stepmother. Some of the men had no coupons and others did not bring a mug or spoon but it didn't matter—everyone got served!

Tan Hoope said did not know there were so many pretty girls looking at Joyce and myself—turning to me asked to accompany him on his rounds—the cheek of him!

Half past five left the stall to join Dad and the others. Later there was dancing—sideshows with fortune-telling doing very well—guess we all wanted our fortunes told!

The men enjoyed themselves though they were disappointed at not being allowed in the cells. The three hours passed very quickly when the bell was rung to announce that the time was up.

I think I shall sleep well tonight—exhausted!

Saturday, 3 April 1943

Rained all morning, the Nips are irritable today—water turned off—no steam— and tea at about 9.30 a.m. Men not allowed to bring in the supper and we had to queue in the Rose Garden for it. The Men's Orchestral Concert was also cancelled. A real rotten day after yesterday! The war must be going bad for the Japs was the general consensus!

Wednesday, 7 April 1943

Lady Heath returned. Over 100 men (Jews) were interned today and they were put in the Old Rice Store. Have been advised for an immediate increase in protein consumption and the matter is receiving attention (maybe an extra dog or two!!!) The Jap authorities have increased our salt ration to 20 grams and the vegetable rations to 300 grams per head per day. Received from Japs—1,902 lbs of salt; 2,225 lbs of sugar and 584 lbs of tea—now divide that by (if the whole received this) over 3,500 men, women and children—or between 400 women and children—whichever way you look at it—not much to sustain us!

Thursday, 8 April 1943

Dad's birthday and being the meeting day we had the chance to see him—poor Dad, he is looking thinner each time I see him ...

Thursday, 22 April 1943

Dr Williams spoke to us at 8.30 p.m. about Mr Asahi's farewell speech. Miss Parfitt then read out the results of the Literary Competition. Imagine my astonishment when I hear 'E. Bromley' called out—that's the nom-de-plume I used for the story I wrote. I had won a special prize—1 lb tin of peaches, and I had forgotten that I had entered in the competition. Mrs Keets remarked afterwards that Miss Parfitt could not have succeeded to astonish them more even if she had dropped a bomb in their midst when she read out 'In the short story section, a special prize is awarded to E. Bromley and I may safely let out that it is a nom-de-plume of our youngest entrant, Sheila Allan. Well done!'

Congratulations all round and I really felt that I'd be glad if the concrete would open up and swallow me—it's so embarrassing and all I could do was mumble 'thank you'.

Literary Competition: From the Report by the Chairman (Mr H. Weisberg)

This competition has I am glad to say, evoked more interest than its sponsors had counted upon. There were altogether no less than 120 entries so that from a quantitative point of view, the competition has been an unqualified success.

I shall leave it to Reverend Colin King to address you in a few moments on the qualitative aspect and shall confine myself to telling you how the judges went about their work.

You may be interested to know how many entries were spread over the different categories.

In section (a) Short Stories ... there were 26 serious, 8 humorous, 2 detective and 3 ghost stories.

In section (b) Essays ... there were 11 serious and 3 light.

In section (c) Verse ... there were 25 serious and 28 light.

In section (d) there were 14 one-act plays.

From the Adjudicators' Report by Reverend Colin King

I have been asked to present the Report of the Adjudicators on the entries submitted in the Literary Competition and in a moment I shall deal with them class by class. Speaking first of the entries as a whole, however, I think it correct to say that few were excellent or even open competitive standard.

At the same time the great majority showed evidence of having been written with sincerity and with considerable forethought. Nothing that we read bore signs of genius and in some classes we did not feel justified in recommending the award of any prize, because we were of the opinion that we must require a higher standard than good intentions and industry alone could achieve ...

Class 1 ... Short Stories—was subdivided under headings—serious, humorous, detective and ghost. To the 'serious' section we awarded two ordinary prizes and *one special prize*, the last being *awarded partly in consideration of the youth of the authoress, and partly because the story fell rather into a class by itself. It possessed real merit and the award was held unanimously to be thoroughly warranted by the quality of the work.* On the other hand, the generally inferior quality of the entries in the other three 'short story sections' and the limited number of entries of 'detective' and 'ghost' stories, caused us to give but one prize for the three classes together ...

Class A differentiated, as I have said, four categories of short stories—serious, humorous, detective and ghost.

A common failing in this class was inability to recognise that a short story is a definite literary genre; and that diary material or plain narrative alone (whether actual or fictional) does not constitute a short story unless it has been smelted and forged to shape by the craftsmanship of an artist.

There were many writers of short stories who clearly did not realise this.

They wrote long anecdotes or episodes; narrative that was sincere, interesting, in some cases, linguistically competent in most but their entries lacked any tension between personalities, conflict of purpose, or striving of circumstance against circumstance. A short story must be a literary whole, with beginning, end and progress from one to the other. A piece of mere narrative—say an interesting journey or a slice of biography or autobiography—may contain great merit, but it does not, by itself, constitute a short story ...

The remarks which I have made may, perhaps, serve to lead some of those who entered to self-criticism of present blemishes with an assurance that there was interest in what they wrote and that greater experience would enable many to write work which would afford genuine pleasure to readers as well as real satisfaction to the writers. If such satisfaction proceed from a justified confidence that it is based on ability to practise an artist's craft, those who have attained to it will neither desire other reward, nor lack it.

Now the story ... 1st story written in Changi on 19th January, 1943

Motherless Eileen

A solitary figure stood on the rocks watching the great golden dawn, for sunrise at the seaside possessed witchery and glories which filled the heart of this early watcher with adoration and called forth from her lips exultant anthems of praise.

Eileen Carey was a tall, quiet girl with a fair clear complexion and grave, wistful brown eyes. Her thick dark hair grew in wavy masses and surrounded her ears with becoming tendrils of soft curls. Her face was tender and full of charm while her fingers were very slender and white that denoted her sensitiveness and artistic nature.

As she gazed at the flushed sky, her eyes which held a singular fascination in their mild sparkling depths, were now filled with a tender, loving light and childish gladness. She was thinking of the letter she had written to Edna Harman, the doctor's wife and was anxiously waiting to see the result her letter would bring.

An hour later she sat with Gloria Lorimer and her parents at breakfast. 'You were up early,' inquired Olga Lorimer, a good-looking woman with delicate features, golden hair and very dark blue eyes. 'Oh! don't you know, she is a nature worshipper,' answered Gloria, her eighteen year old daughter and looked at Eileen with a knowing grin on her pretty face but Eileen only smiled and held her peace for this act of hers was commented upon nearly every morning, besides, Gloria could not see what there was to be admired at such an early hour of the morning. Her father, Robert Lorimer was a quiet man, more interested in his papers than the subject of getting up early.

That evening Eileen received a note from Edna Harman, inviting her to come and see her, and in a state of nervous excitement she got ready to go.

Eileen was two years older than Gloria and had known the Lorimers since she was fifteen. She was an orphan left to the care of a boarding school where she met Gloria who become so fond of her that when she left school a year ago she insisted that Eileen should stay with her as her companion. Being an only child and spoilt at that she got her wish.

A week after her arrival at the house she met Edna Harman and her husband, a clever doctor, who was the family doctor as well as their adviser. The day she set eyes on that beautiful woman five years ago, she had fallen and been in love with her ever since.

At fifty-two Edna Harman was a strikingly beautiful woman with perfectly proportioned slenderness, her skin was the transparent glow of health and she had light blue eyes with the glint of steel in them. Her brown curly hair streaked grey and her graceful carriage gave her an air of distinction that was the more marked because of her lack of self-consciousness. Her voice was full of charming inflections.

Dr John Harman and his wife were very devoted to each other and the loss of their eighteen year old daughter two years ago made them love each other more than ever. It was a terrible blow and they had not got completely over it.

As time went by, the friendship between Edna Harman and Eileen grew and blossomed into one of the most beautiful friendships that could be imagined. The former was one of those women who had the power of reading people and was a fine judge of character. She saw that Eileen was not really happy and that there was something lacking in her life. Often she had found her gazing at her in rapt admiration and a sad strange look in her eyes which she was unable to define.

A year ago she became very ill and Eileen had asked permission to nurse her. Those three months paved the way for Eileen to enter the hearts of Dr Harman and his wife.

Her last evening with them was a sad one and Edna made a discovery. Eileen had entered her room and with a book on her lap she sat gazing at her, thinking that she was sleeping. The thought of leaving her rose and swept over the girl's heart bringing a touching expression of patient sorrow to her face and giving a far-away wistful look to the beautiful eyes where tears often gathered but very rarely fell. With a quick and graceful movement she suddenly went on her knees beside the supposed sleeping Edna and whispered low. 'Mother, I love you.' There was a note of anguish and suffering as she uttered those words and kissing the face on the pillow gently so as not to wake the patient she left the room. It was then that Edna discovered the truth.

Eileen was an only child and had not known a mother's love when she needed it. Her mother died a few days after she was born and her father put her in a boarding school at the early age of three and a half. That very day he met with an accident and the result was that she was left alone and was taken care of by the kind teachers who found her to be a very lovable child.

Fate brought Edna Harman into her life and the girl for the first time realised that she had never known what it was to have a mother. She saw in Edna the qualities of a good mother and had instantly recognised and felt the motherly heart of that woman. She became her ideal mother who aroused and brought to life the craving for a mother's love and the need of one. This was the girl's secret which she kept to herself for five years—which had burst forth from her lips a year ago and which she had revealed in her letter to Edna the day before.

Edna Harman knew Eileen would come that evening and was looking forward to it, for she knew she was on the verge of entering a lonely and forsaken garden and that she was to be the chief gardener to clear away the weeds and put in their place the roses and flowers of joy and happiness.

There came a knock at the door. Edna opened it to admit a flushed looking girl with a lovely bouquet of roses which she gave to her. Receiving the flowers with a charming smile, she invited her to enter while she put them away.

When she returned she found the girl standing at the window. 'Well, my dear?' she began and extended her hands which were caught by the girl and they found themselves in each other's arms. Moved by this mutual action she gently said, 'Tell me what is in your heart—I will understand'. Little by little Eileen poured her heart out to the motherly and sympathetic listener.

'Poor child, why didn't you tell me earlier instead of keeping it so long concealed in your heart? Were you afraid of me?' she asked.

'In a way, yes, although I love you and find you good and noble, yet I wasn't sure whether you would be pleased with the knowledge that I love you. I am a stranger and mean nothing to you—but I could not continue like this any longer—I had to tell you. That is why I wrote and dreading all the while the consequences of such a letter,' then taking her hands, she continued in a shy pleading tone, 'Mother, will you let me have this privilege of calling you thus. Be such a one to me and love me a little.'

For a second Edna looked away—the girl had touched her by such an appeal.

'Yes,' came the soft reply for the memory of her own daughter called forth all her love for this motherless girl and their eyes met in perfect understanding. It would be difficult to describe Eileen's thoughts and emotions as she went home. The soul cannot at once translate itself perfectly in words and there are 'thoughts without words', which to every being are the prelude of both supreme joy and sorrow.

From that day, life was different for Eileen Carey and every evening she was with Edna Harman. It seemed as if they were always together. Every day brought its conversation and with each evening, love on both sides grew.

A year had glided swiftly by since that day. Gloria was engaged to be married to Gerald Rowland, a young banker of athletic build—a good-looking, likeable young man filled with the zest of life. Eileen still lived in the same house but her heart was with Dr Harman and his wife.

Then came the day of the wedding and Dr Harman made plans to adopt Eileen now that Gloria no longer needed a companion. When Eileen went to see them, Dr Harman left his wife to deal with the matter which she did so without much ado.

'Eileen, my dear, now that Gloria is married I wonder if you'd like to stay with us and look after two lonely old people who love you. You have called me "Mother" for all these months—I would like you to do so for the rest of your life. Be our own daughter for we need you now. Think about it and give me your answer soon,' Edna spoke softly but with emotion. In an equally soft voice Eileen gave her answer, 'Mother, I don't need to think about it and nothing would please me more. May you never regret what you are giving me—your love.'

At this moment a tall slenderly built man in his fifties with serious blue eyes, thinking that everything would be settled by that time, entered. Eileen stood up and went to him. Flinging her arms around his neck, she kissed him affectionately and said, 'Darling Dad, you are an angel and I love you so for giving me this happiness'. Putting his arms around her, he propelled her into a chair and talked the matter over.

It was dawn such as that morning when Eileen had stood watching the glory of the new day. On that same spot now stood Gloria with her husband welcoming the first day of their married life.

Not far away Edna Harman and Eileen too were watching the dawn. 'My love,' whispered Edna, 'we'll begin life anew together—loving and helping each other we'll trudge bravely along the pathway of life.'

Another figure was walking towards them and Dr Harman joined these two. They were silently happy and neither spoke a word for it was their sacred hour. Thus they stood watching the flow of the rising sun. The morning air smelt sweet and there was a gentle breeze blowing, the waves dashed ceaselessly along the beach—everything spelt calm and peace. It was only the beginning and promised a happy future for the three watchers.

Special prize—1 lb tin of Peaches (Just beginner's luck!)

Tuesday, 27 April 1943

Dr Johns has been asked to resign by the Nips and elections taking place. For the present Mr Wallace is acting Head Commandant. Went to see Mrs Gregory-

Jones and had an enjoyable chit-chat. Mrs Loveridge has been elected Fatigue Officer on the resignation of Miss Egger.

A sentry is now stationed in a new position at the end of the road leading to the prison. We are asked to note that another bow is required. Miss Griff has retired from the post of announcer and Judy Good has taken on the job. The winner of the R. Walker picture raffle was Miss S. Early. Camp Credit is now $4 instead of $5. There is also shortage of sugar ration and we are advised to go slow with our ration. We now get the extra protein diet of herring every second day and eggs twice a week and extra vitamins in our soup as a supply of green beans have become available—hurrah!

After all this I failed to mention that we have been allowed to attend religious services in the courtyard.

For the Roman Catholic—mass is celebrated at 8 a.m. by Father Moran, turnabout by Father Cosgrave.

We have several ministers such as Major Harvey, Reverend A.J. Bennett, Reverend W.R. Bales and Reverend Tyler Thompson and others willing to conduct services.

It is good that we are allowed to worship our God in here . . .

30 April 1943   Good Friday
Had an entertaining Shakespeare Night organised by Miss Parfitt.

From Pow-Wow

On the retirement of Mr Johns, by order of the Nipponese authorities, Mr Adrian Clark was elected head of the Men's Camp. A letter has been sent to Mr Johns thanking him for all he did for the Women's Camp during his tenure of office.

The Women's Camp received permission to resume walks outside the gates three times a week.

It is reported there may be a shortage of sugar; people are advised to use their ration carefully.

The dietitians have decided, for the time being, to continue the extra protein diet of herring every other day and eggs twice weekly, as this is considered necessary. There will also be a certain amount of extra vitamins in the soup as a supply of green beans have been obtained.

Monday, 3 May 1943
Rain, rain and more rain—did it come down this morning but oh! so refreshing after days of humid weather. Have taken to sleeping outside with Miss Foss and Pansy—am afraid we spend talking late into the night!

Sometimes I look up at the sky—clear sky—and that Milky Way—how I wish I am up there looking down and seeing women and children sleeping every which way and I ponder what is to become of us—how much longer can we stand being here and with each other. Already there are cracks in our community. Starvation, dysentery, beri-beri and malaria—just about everything is slowly taking its toll on our integrity especially when we see our loved ones slowly fading away.

Would we sell ourselves?—I don't know—maybe there are cases but who are we to judge morally—can we honestly say that but 'For the Grace of God' there go I?

Judge not and you will not be judged but it is not easy to look into our hearts and be big enough to say 'I understand'!

This is war and war seems to change people and being in here in close proximity to other human beings can easily destroy our good intentions.

I look around me and take in everything that goes on—I look at the people here and the friends that I have made—friends like Jeannie Summers, Mary Winters, Joyce Edwards and Nellie Symons—all around my age—we are in this together and we depend on each other to boost our morale and strange to say we seem to be blessed with a sense of humour!

Tuesday, 4 May 1943
Men's quartet and the Choir came over to play selections from Gilbert and Sullivan Operas in the Rose Garden at 7.15 p.m. What a gala evening it was—imagine the women in their latest styles bedecked in jewels and furs and men in 'Top Hats and Tails'—well! we can let our imagination run riot, can't we?

The Changi Orchestra conducted by Maestro Crofts played selections from 'The Yeoman of the Guard' and the 'Gondoliers'. The Camp Choir gave forth renditions from 'Patience', 'Ruddigore', 'Trial by Jury' and 'The Pirates of Penzance'.

The music and singing was really something. Loved every minute of it and all too soon the show came to an end.

On a sad note—our two men are still in confinement but now made more comfortable. Allowed food and water, a book each and two camp beds. Men staying outside brought in again but fatigues working as usual. Walks permitted but not for the men. Women not allowed to speak to any man—only two women who wear the armbands. Next day armbands were issued to the others—rules regarding them must be strictly observed. Camp coupons cannot be carried over to next month! Each month different coloured coupons. Some material came in from International Red Cross and given to those in most need. Sardines and bully beef are being supplied by International Red Cross collected in Singapore. The Fatigue Officer will be in the Carpenter's Shop daily from 9.15 a.m. to 9.45 a.m.

The Jewish community gave a quantity of bread for the children. And members of different nationalities are asked to choose their own representatives.

Friday, 7 May 1943
Happy birthday to Dr Hopkins—had birthday in Carpenter's Shop. Dr Hopkins looked 'super' in what looked like an evening dress of a dark red silk sarong, a sun-top and a black sash around her waist complete with red 'tromphers' [sandals]! Someone played the piano and the party was in full swing when Mrs Barbour came in and said 'If you want to see something really beautiful, just go outside and look at the sky'. I went out and behold!—what did I see?—No, not our planes flying overhead! The sky was all awash with colour—beautiful and delicately tinged with colours beyond human conception. To make it complete there were two rainbows stretching across the sky. Yet with all this beautiful unique colouring there were grey clouds of a storm gathering behind all this beauty. Many came out and gazed in silent rapture—it was simply beyond words—how could you describe such artistry! No one, no matter how great a painter, could colour the sky as it was this evening—could capture on canvas even half of the radiance and hues. That perfect blue, the vibrant orange, the subtle mauve and the blush of pink—who can blend these colours so harmoniously, and who can paint these ominous clouds of approaching storm without spoiling the beauty of the sky? God, the Great Painter is the only one, the Perfect Painter who with just a stroke of His paintbrush across the sky can produce such a magnificent picture . . .

Friday, 21 May 1943
Got up this morning feeling rotten—violently sick last night with tummy pains. Mrs Milne saw me heaving my guts out and immediately carted me here (hospital). Head feels as if someone has a sledge-hammer constantly on it. Temperature up to 104°—body aching—I can't see—I can't hear! God, what's happening? I feel so—oh, no—Nurse—help—God—

Saturday, 22 May 1943
I want to die—Dear God, why, why. What are you doing to me? I feel my head is split open—I can't write properly—am I going blind? If I have to go through this every couple of weeks—I'd rather die—God, let me die now—I can't go on. Here comes the doctor—

Friday, 28 May 1943

Feeling more human after last entry—did I really write all that? I feel so weak and washed out. Did not see the Changi Show—I believe it was very good. Managed to get the cutting from Pow-Wow—'Each Changi show increases our wonder and amazement and Friday night's Barbour-Kronin cabaret was no exception. The energy, work, ingenuity and invention that was evident left one speechless . . .'

Monday, 31 May 1943

I'm sick of bed—I want to leave the hospital—when am I going to be allowed out? Have been having visitors now that I'm on the mend again. Billie James was admitted last night with pains—hope she is not going to suffer as much as I did—I wouldn't want to wish all that pain on my worst enemy! Allowed to walk a bit—that's good news.

Tuesday, 1 June 1943

Another bad night. Mrs Orr had fits of coughing and kept the whole ward awake.

Dr Scott MacGregor came this afternoon to get a blood sample—applied some icy stuff (probably spirit of some sort) on the tip of my finger (middle finger of my right hand) stabbed a sharp needle into it once (Dr Worth on the other side of the bed watching) then from a small case took out a long glass tube with a rubber tube attached at one end. With the glass tube pressed on the little pool of blood he sucked the blood with the rubber one—then he sucked a purple liquid stuff from a small bottle, shook the tube to mix the two. After this he brought out two strips of glass—with one he placed it on my finger and having got the blood on it, he rubbed it onto the other strip—did this twice. Wonder what he is going to test these for.

Wednesday, 2 June 1943

Was rudely woken up by Betty Burn—very excited—said something going on—a naval battle! Almost shared in her excitement and forgave her for waking me up—then found out it was only thunder and lightning in the distance—what a fizzer!!!

Thursday, 3 June 1943

Saw Dad today—had heard some men shut up in the tower—asked Dad if he knew anything—said the Japs found some women passing food and drinks to the men while practising on their instruments—asked which they prefer—'Women or music' and they answered 'Both' so he said follow me and he locked them up in the tower—one man fainted. Said he wrote to Auntie Grace and told her that we had no fresh meat, bread, fish, fruit and vegetables by writing down the names of the only butcher, baker, fishmonger and greengrocer in the little village in Australia where the family lived—only those who have been to that little village will understand what he means—what a clever idea! Mrs Woods admitted in the ward again and looking very sick. Am still feeling weak from all that diarrhoea and high temperature.

Saturday, 5 June 1943

Came out of hospital yesterday—have to take it easy for a few days and build up strength before going back to work. Order from the Japs—forbidden to play any games, musical instruments or any other form of gaiety because General So and So is being buried today. Wish this headache would go away. Getting some things from the International Red Cross. Having daily issue of maize bread and fresh fruit. Oh bliss! we have a new piano in the Carpenter's Shop!!! Meetings of married people are now allowed. *Now* we have Syonan [Japanese] news broadcasts daily in the Rose Garden at 10.10 p.m. And we are reminded of the order to stand to attention when the Nipponese National Anthem is played and the guards will be watching! Half the Camp attends 128 classes in the Changi 'University'—most popular class—languages!

Friday, 11 June 1943

Nips came round last night between 12 and 1—a little worrying and quickly hid diary between other school books—have to be careful—always—the Japs are getting restless! Mrs Davidson asked if I would like to look after her baby from 9–10 a.m. and 2–2.30 p.m. and 6–7 p.m. Willing to pay and promises that if we leave here she would have me with her as long as I wish to stay with her. Told her I don't want money for something I'd enjoy doing and I can still carry on with my Camp chores.

Monday, 14 June 1943

Miss Marion Aiken aged 73 quietly passed away in the Camp Hospital this morning. She was such a cheerful person and always willing to listen to us young ones. I'm going to miss her talking about her young days. Enjoying looking after Jennifer—she is such a happy little girl—Mrs Davidson insists on $5 cash each month. A number of chickens have been disappearing and we have had unusual meals lately—Watched the Badminton match—what a finish!

Monday, 21 June 1943

Mrs Nixon elected Camp Commandant. Lady Thomas doing VAD work in the San—later fell down stairs and hurt herself.

Thursday, 24 June 1943

For the last couple of nights, the Nips have been on the prowl! Now gates and doors are to be left open throughout the night and they do not want to be escorted round! We are asked to hand in—tin hats, daggers, stilettos, binoculars and whistles—strange items surely! Had them around accompanied by the Sikhs to examine our things in the cells—took away some books, candles, electrical appliances and photos and cameras—took my camera—but my school books were left undisturbed—I was sick in the stomach when I saw them enter our cell. Told books will be returned after they were examined and stamped.

Tonight at 8.30–9.30 in the Carpenter's Shop—'Midsummer Madness' a Children's party for the grown-ups! Put on your rompers and bibs—bring your nanny if you like—all games you used to play like Oranges and Lemons—Ring a Ring O Rosy—Musical chairs, etc. No children under 15—all adults must be under 10! The party was a huge success and everyone had a great time being young again!

Saturday, 3 July 1943

This evening put on the 'Circus' for the men in the main courtyard—the show was a *Howling* success—the men laughed at the clowns and animal antics—the Camp Orchestra was exceptionally good. It's grand to hear the men laughing and enjoying themselves. By all accounts the Jap sentries enjoyed the show.

Monday, 5 July 1943

Relatives' meeting—saw Dad—not at all well—I'm worried about him—had a long talk—spoke about the past—wanted to know if I remembered much about our early years on the mines in Siam—and thinking about it brings to mind images of the place—I remember going there on my school holidays—I'd get there by boat and stayed overnight at the halfway house. Next day I'd travel on the sampan poled along by two Siamese men—the sampan had a roof to protect us from the sun. The journey took four hours to get to Paktak, our destination. Dad was there to meet me and together we'd ride on a trolley worked by hand along the lines to the village. Our house stood beside a lake—a large house—Dad's bedroom at one end and where I slept, the other end. We each had a bathroom at the end but the toilet was outside at the back. The main house had a walkway across a chasm to the cook house where the Chinese cook and my Chinese Amah had rooms of their own. We had a wide verandah along the front of the house. At twilight we'd close all doors and windows and quietly stayed inside and before long there'd be pad, pad along the verandah with occasional muffled growls—the tiger was on the prowl—I'd watch him through the cracks—what a magnificent creature! He'd take a turn on the verandah and then down the steps and off into the darkness till the same time again the next night. Remembered the time when Dad found a snake curled under his pillow! Had to watch for cobras too. There was another house behind us—another European miner lived there on his own. The manager had the big house on the top of the hill facing ours. I remember those steps going up the hill to visit the family. But the best picture of all was the lake—often I'd be in a little boat and rowed around it and once I got lost but I was able to find my way back—Dad was worried as it was getting late in the afternoon. He was cross with me and I wasn't allowed to use the boat for a week.

I told him about what I remembered and he began to cry which upset me greatly. 'You must have been a lonely little girl,' he said, 'I didn't spend much time with you, did I?' 'But I wasn't lonely Dad—I had plenty to occupy me and I loved it there' I told him. He was going to say something else but time was up and we had to go. Oh, Dad, please don't be sad and take care of yourself.

Friday, 9 July 1943

Had another piano recital at 8.30 p.m. in the Carpenter's Shop. Xenia has a lovely voice—she sang four songs accompanied by Mrs Milne. It was raining but the sound of the rain and the music together made a most soothing harmony. I particularly liked Xenia singing 'Danny Boy' and 'Plaisir d'Amour'.

Margaret Young played the study in F Minor, Jesu Joy of My Desiring (Bach); Sonata in G (Beethoven); Waltzes in A Flat and E Minor (Chopin—my favourite); and a piece I haven't heard before The little white donkey (Ibert). All in all it was a happy interlude in our ordinary course of Camp life.

Wednesday, 14 July 1943

There was a fight between two women today over one woman calling another a 'prostitute'—talk about a slinging match! They went 'hammer and tongs' as the saying goes and calling each other names. Then someone joined in and got badly hit on the head. Mrs Lund, in trying to separate the fighters, got bitten on the arm. One of them collapsed and was taken to hospital. Her mother, in a fit of hysteria, ran to the office and reported the affair to the Nips. The end result— Diana and Betty were locked in a cell and Mrs Nixon had to stay with them.

Thursday, 15 July 1943
At 6.30 p.m. we had the men's musical concert (piano, flute and violin) performed by Mr Gluhoff and Mr Syde Ross (flute and violin solos); Mr Eisinger and Mr Edyvean gave us a duet on two pianos. They arrived late but were allowed their full time—an enjoyable evening.

There are to be no lights between 9 a.m. and 8 p.m. except in bad weather. We are now receiving two ounces of tea per person. Stripe material to be used in the hospital and what's left to be sold in the store at $1.15 per yard. And we have also been given more material for the children, girls and boys.

We've been seeing some cats about—they better be careful—if they stay, there may not be any cats!!!

Sunday, 18 July 1943
Saw Dr Hopkins up and about early this morning—found out later she was trying to make marmalade jam!

The sunrise this morning was spectacular and always it seems there is a rainbow about.

Tomorrow our Relatives' Meetings in the Rose Garden have been extended.

Also we've had the Nips visiting us four times today. Have to be very, very careful with everything. So far, nobody knows that I am keeping a diary.

Did we have an impromptu concert the other day?—the Creche ladies did! They arrived to find their chairs and seats placed in a row all facing one way across the corridor. Morris Junior and May Stuart got the other children to sit down and the show was on the way. Junior and May did an excellent imitation of Mrs Kronin's Indian Dance. Poor Genevieve Logan could hardly constrain herself—she had to join in the dance. They were so serious and intent and their graceful mimicking was delightful to watch. The dancers then stopped, faced the audience, bowed and began to clap. The audience comprising of two adults and the rest of the children joined in the clapping. Encouraged, the dancers gave a repeat performance again and again with more applause started by May and Junior until all tired of the game. Ah! the innocence of children! They do take notice of what goes on around them and we must be made aware of the fact that they do imitate what they see!

Wednesday, 21 July 1943
Bathing picnic today and am looking forward to that. It rained very heavily last night. I slept on the table under the showers with Xenia and Nellie. Being on the outer side I got fairly wet but it was still better than sleeping in the cell when it's 'muggy'. Had a strange dream and told Miss Smith about it. She reckoned

it meant some good things are going to be in store for us—I wonder! Asked her if she got her shoes—'Oh yes! I went to the Office for them. The So-So told me that I hadn't put my name down on the list. I told the So-So I did put my name down and I wasn't going to go without them. "You are a very determined young woman" was the comment. "Oh yes and not so young either" but I got my shoes!'

Came back from swimming—it was really great—the day was not too hot, the water lovely and cold. I had lessons in lifesaving and we kept within bounds this time—a most enjoyable time was had by all. Saw Mrs Gordon—she's looking much better.

Tuesday, 27 July 1943

Tonight we had a play written by Dr Elliot and Mrs Taplyn and produced by Mrs Kennard. It was performed in the Carpenter's Shop at 8.30 p.m. It was called 'The Snatcher'—a sketch on Camp life. Dr Elliot as Miss Tooth who lost her teeth was superb. The Malay Ghost (Miss Helen Latta) was a good imitation of one of the warders in prewar days. Mrs Ackers entered into her part with a band and Mrs Byron as the woman who had second sight was too good to be true. Miss Poppy Rackman who thought all the time of scientific outlook was really a scream. Miss Griff was a real glamour girl in a sun-suit and hair done in the latest fashion. Of course, Dr Hopkins (to me) outbeats the rest in looks and bearing in the housecoat she made. Congratulations to all—we enjoyed the show and the actresses had their own party after the show.

Thursday, 29 July 1943

Miss Foss in hospital.

Friday, 30 July 1943

This morning everything seems quiet. As I write this with the light slowly fading, I hear faintly in the distance the sound of a dripping tap. It disturbs my concentration. Drip, drip, drip—it goes on and on. I don't know where it is coming from but it beats into my brain and I can't think. I'll have to give up—that drip, drip is getting on my nerves!

Saturday, 31 July 1943

What a night! That dripping tap just went on and on. I don't know if anybody else heard it or was it my imagination! Perhaps that's how prisoners have to put up with that sort of torture and torture it was! I had my fingers in my ears, I buried my head under my pillow but to no avail—I could still hear that drip, drip, drip!

Maude, Mrs Davidge and Mary Lowe are down with the 'flu'. As a matter of fact Mrs Davidge had to go to hospital. Glad to say Miss Foss is much better.

[A Fantasy]

An announcement was made in the queues but I was not present. Later I was told that M [Dr Hopkins] was going to be beaten in the Rose Garden at two that afternoon. I refused to believe the news thinking that they must have misunderstood the announcement.

At two, the whole floor was as quiet as a mouse. I ran down the steps with the tormenting thought that it could be true. The iron steps resounded loudly as I ran. Along the corridors the whole Camp was waiting—for what? I asked someone 'Tell me what's going on?' She put her hands on my shoulder saying, 'I'm sorry' and burst into tears. That was too much for me, sick with dread, I arrived at the garden gate.

What I saw, drained the colour from my face—my beloved M tied to a post. Not far away three Japs were sitting and talking to a sentry who held a whip in his hand.

Heedless of the cries and hands that stretched out to stop me, I rushed forward. As I neared that horrible post, M commanded me to stay away. I heeded it not and flung myself and embraced her. 'Mother, Mother' I sobbed with anguish and fear. A hand on my shoulder to try and pull me away. Instinctively I encircled M with my arms and clasped my own hands firmly round the post.

Love seemed to give me strength to resist the sentry's hand. My arms and hands were like bands of iron firmly locked together, my eyes dilated with pain and fear.

The Japs got impatient and told the sentry to get on with the whipping. I braced myself. The blows came—stinging, smarting, into my flesh. I felt the hot tears down my cheeks—again, again and again the whip was at work. I closed my eyes—involuntarily I winced as I tasted blood. Her body was also bruised but my body broke the force of those vicious blows.

The minutes seemed to drag. My head throbbed dangerously. My body felt like a mangled corpse.

At last it was over. The Japs left us drenched in our own blood. Someone came and untied M's hands and I simply passed out! The next thing I knew I found myself in bed and bandaged like a corpse fit for a coffin. I remembered what happened. I looked around and saw another bandaged figure in the bed beside me.

Could all this take place? Or is my imagination running away with me? This place is getting me down and I must not think along those lines. And if the Japs find this I think I could be in a bit of a spot. I must not write any more in this vein. I'm becoming morbid—I must stop!

Sunday, 1 August 1943

Had news that Dad has gone into hospital. Dr Worth said not to worry too much but I know it's more than that. He hasn't been well for weeks but refuses to see the docs. I noticed his legs swelling up and he had difficulty with his breathing. I hope the doctor keeps him in hospital for a while.

Tuesday, 3 August 1943

Saw Dad yesterday at our usual meeting. Shocked to see a marked change since I saw him a fortnight ago. Said had a high temperature Friday night—he felt so sick that he went to see the doctor but fainted on the way and woke up in hospital. Later learned that two men had found him unconscious and had carried him to the hospital. The doctor's report—'tummy trouble, flu and clotted blood in his head'. Dr Del Tufo asked Adrian Clarke about him doing some light chores. Glennie I'm told, is very good with Dad—washing and looking after his needs. I'm glad he's got someone in the Men's Camp to keep an eye on him.

Mrs Cornelius suggests I write to Dad and also to Glennie for report on his progress.

Tuesday, 10 August 1943

Nineteen today! Mrs Freddy Bloom wants me to have 'elevenses' with her—a little shy I told her that she'd better be warned about the 'little dumb chick' she's invited. 'Oh! That would be a change!' she said in that delightful Canadian voice of hers. Got up early for a shower—guess what! there was no water this morning but it came on a couple of hours later. Had to get the washing done first so was late at the 'elevenses' . . . Everyone seemed to be talking at once. Mrs Bloom and Mrs de Mowbray told me where they were and what they did when they were nineteen. The former was still at college. She felt quite grown-up on account of her height but was very self-conscious about her long nose! Mrs de Mowbray was nursing in 1917—she was extremely shy and childish in many ways. She has three children, the youngest is twelve and the eldest twenty-three. Received flowers from Dad, Glennie and 'Uncle' Phil.

Dr Worth wasn't feeling too good—had one tooth out and two filled.

The water was turned off again this afternoon.

Wednesday, 11 August 1943

Last night Joyce, Nellie and myself did not go to bed until well after midnight. I made them laugh with my funny tricks. I was in a crazy mood!

For the first time Bloom and de Mowbray slept out in the garden—an umbrella was on their chair. Around three this morning it rained—I had to sleep in the school room. Bloom slept right through till morning. Jokingly I blamed her for the rain on account of the umbrella being an invitation for it to rain!

Our Monday night lectures are a real treat—Mr Gibson-Hill on Evolution of Modern Man.

Earthquakes and Volcanoes by Dr Ingham.

Lecture on Graphology by Mr Scott and I guess we'll all be giving the noticeboard a once over!

Our Sunday services continue to inspire us—we are indeed lucky not to have them cancelled.

Friday, 13 August 1943

There was a strange row going on at about six this morning on AIV . . . Mrs B poked Mrs L with an umbrella with the words 'You are disturbing everyone with your snores'. At this, the latter opened her eyes and said 'Nonsense, I wasn't asleep' and entered her cell to see the time. Came out and told Mrs B 'It's nearly six and it's time to get up anyway'.

Just then Mrs D came out and baptised Mrs B saying 'This will teach you not to wake us up at this hour of the morning'. As a result, Mrs B is going to complain to Mrs N.

Camp Lullaby
(with apologies)

You might have been the best internee
And first rate at every chore,
Had the temper of an angel
And were brilliant furthermore.
All your goodness counted for nothing,
All your virtues we ignored,
For the only thing that mattered
Was, my lady, did you snore?

You might have swiped your neighbour's ration,
Stole wristwatches by the score,
Stuck bent pins in dear old ladies
And bounced babies on the floor.

We judged you not your blooming morals
Though they shocked us to the core.
Rest assured, all was forgiven
Just as long you did not snore!

Saturday, 14 August 1943

A strange phenomenon occurred on AIV this morning . . . 'You brute! You Pig! How dare you! What . . .' Mrs B gave vent in her sleep but what followed was too dramatically sudden that it could not have been a nightmare. She got up, gathered her things and disappeared into her cell. What a life! What a woman! We were left wondering what it was all about.

Shopping day. Bought some things—the second time after many, many months.

The water was turned off again. Rehearsing—I'm Tubal in the 'Merchant of Venice'. Raining again.

Monday, 16 August 1943

Rehearsal of the 'Water Babies'. Joyce, Nellie and self went to the Rose Garden to practise the dance this afternoon. Morning had a game of quoits.

Tuesday, 17 August 1943

Practice, practice all this afternoon. Had an interested audience—four men in the alleyway including a couple of the sentries.

Tit-bit—overheard at first-aid practice—

Instructor: 'What would you do if a patient stopped breathing?'

Pupil: 'Apply artificial repatriation' laughter from the class.

Oh, boy!

Wednesday, 18 August 1943

The show must go on tonight instead as scheduled for tomorrow night—orders from the Nipponese officer. Fathers of those taking part will be allowed in to see the show. It went off very well. Our visitors certainly enjoyed themselves. After the show the Nips came round with a 'lady' friend (perhaps to see that we didn't sneak one of our men in our cells!)

M sleeping outside under the lines.

Cholera injections to take place as from today.

Thursday, 19 August 1943

Joyce and self (nicknamed 'The Twins'!) slept outside again. Arm is sore from the injection. Played quoits after our work. Rested in the afternoon.

8 p.m. . . . Nip officer and two guards appeared on the scene. He looked cross—very cross indeed. Something must have upset him. He kicked the doors opened, pulled the curtains aside, pushed tables and chairs aside and slapped several women as he went on a rampage—like a mad bull, he was. Mrs N and others said he was drunk—sure—drunk with rage was what I thought. Perhaps he received bad news about the war. Poor Joyce, she was quite scared about the whole thing—I think we all were.

Saturday, 21 August 1943
Heard Dr E.S. Lawrie died around 6 this morning—suicide apparently. Afternoon in the Red Cross Hut saw many nurses and doctors attending the funeral. I wonder how many more will go the same way? Sometimes it isn't easy to be cheerful—especially when the 'bug' hits you and you feel as if your inside is coming out in bits and pieces.

Dear God, please end this war soon and get us out of here before we slowly die from hunger.

Thursday, 26 August 1943
Another spell in hospital—feeling rotten—no appetite! Got into trouble for not eating the 'bubo'—horrible stuff! The doc warned if I don't eat the stuff I'll end up getting beri-beri! I don't think I'll want to look at 'watery rice' when I leave this hellhole of a place. Still losing weight—won't win in a Beauty Contest—I look at myself and what do I see—tummy that sticks out—arms and legs—well, I think a spider's legs would look thicker than mine. Skin yellow with 'atebrin'—yak! indeed and don't laugh.

A new literary competition has been arranged on the same lines as the last one held in the spring of this year . . .

Sunday, 29 August 1943
Saw M. Had a talk about the competition—thinks I should have another go at it but am not too sure this time even though have been doing some short stories and having a try at verses—not too good at that either but it helps to while away the time! Went to Church as usual. Signed up for play reading—outside the walls. The programme was most interesting:– 'Trifles' by Susan Somebody—I was Mrs Peters, wife of the County Attorney (Dr Worth). The second play was 'The Applecart' by Bernard Shaw. I was King Magnus in that did not finish this one as time was short—to continue next Sunday.

Thursday, 2 September 1943

There is much talk about repatriation again and it is more than possible that before long we will be leaving Malaya.

Copied from Pow-Wow of 1st September, 1943

Many will be leaving never to return again. It will be a sad farewell for there is something about the East and especially about this country that first wins one's heart and then enters one's blood. Before our departure we should personally like to say:— Thank you, Malaya. Thank you for all you have taught and given me. Thank you for introducing me to your strange people and their different philosophies, customs and habits. Thank you for your charming language (mata mata for policemen, Keta sombong for express train). The many coloured sarong, old hammered brass and pewter, the snakelike kris and the birdlike p'rahaus . . . all these you showed me. The Chinese Temple in Penang, the ancient Portuguese Church in Malacca, a sea of rubber trees turning copper and gold, the view from 'The Gap' on a moonlit night, a tin mine seen in flashes of lightning during a storm . . . I won't forget. And there was Pangkor Island where the whole beach moved with the rhythm of the hermit crabs and the Tamil fishermen sang as they hauled in their nets. In your jungle I saw the first black panther and heard the monkey calling to his pack. Off your shore I hooked a barracuda and watched a school of slowly swimming otters. Thank you too for land and weather where one can really watch plants coming up, growing, blossoming, where the seed becomes a tree and gives fruit within twelve months.

During this last year, you gave us warmth and food . . . food for the body from your trees and fields, food for the soul in the beauty of your skies. Goodbye and bless you.

Now, isn't that a lovely article—I doubt whether I could have penned those feelings as well as our editor of the Pow-Wow—the feelings I truly share with her.

Still have problems with water supply but so far nobody has been caught under the shower!

Had our two cholera injections now—arm pretty sore at the moment.

Friday, 3 September 1943

List of those who received letters from 'home' is posted both in A and E blocks. An accident at the fire—Nellie Symons and Betty Lancaster are looking their old selves once more. Miss Eggar's leg is up to its old form. Eunice Hofer can again face the world though her back is still sore. We don't think 'Nick' Nicholson has a relative across the way so there is no telling whom she had in mind when she carefully dehusked her coconut murmuring 'These coconuts are like some of the men; take off their whiskers and there's nothing left'. Speaking of coconuts, what an appetite our tame chicken has! (called Horace by the amateurs but Clementine by those who know!!) An awful lot of scraping goes on in A kitchen and ILA [Isolation Lower A] but it's never too much for him—her—it!

There is one thing wrong with Betty Milne's new novel—she's taking too much time writing it—and we want to know what happened next.

Sunday, 5 September 1943

Church as usual. Evening rehearsal of the 'Merchant of Venice'—I am Tubal, the Irish Jew. Miss Parfitt is coaching me on the 'Merchant of Venice'. Also rehearsing for the Acrobatic Act, Russian and Oriental Dances.

Tuesday, 21 September 1943

Oiled my hair to make greasy curls for tonight—all ready for 'The Merchant of Venice' . . . All went well and everyone enjoyed the show—the first public appearance of the Play Reading Circle!

Thursday, 23 September 1943

Art Exhibition in the Red Cross Hut—had a look—not much knowledge of art but liked some of the portraits. The others I didn't understand—too abstract for me—I like my art plain and simple!

Joyce much better last night. Three new internees arrived today. Blackout on again tonight (8 p.m. to 8 a.m.).

Thursday, 7 October 1943

Have been in hospital again—another bout of malaria. Now coughing has started and have to take things quietly for a while. Feeling very shaky in my legs and no energy left for anything—haven't written since last entry (23rd September). My head feels so sore and I see that beri-beri has set in. Not in too good a shape at the moment.

Sunday, 10 October 1943

Last night we were told that there is going to be a Roll Call in the Rose Garden at 9 a.m. today. Early this morning we got ready to go to the Rose Garden. Felt very uneasy about my diaries—what to do with them—stacked them between the school books and prayed that they'd be safe as before when the Japs came around the last couple of times.

An hour went by before a troop of about 30 men arrived and started searching each cell. I felt quite sick. Another hour went by and we were ordered to go to A garden and E block. It was really hot today—we had rugs across lines for some shade. It wasn't until late in the afternoon we were allowed to go to the Carpenter's Shop. Many fainted and some were sick with the heat—thirsty and hungry—especially the children. Later we were given coffee and tea. Coconuts were opened and eaten and the children had milk brought to them. I felt rotten—still suffering from the effects of malaria and wondering if the Japs found my books. Permission given to cook something. About half-past seven 'All Clear'. Could go back to our cells. Tried to get to my cell as fast as my shaky legs would go but nothing was disturbed in ours—it was just as we had left it this morning. Food arrived—rice and soup— new batch of men—no guards with them this time. Felt too ill to eat and had a fit of the shivers again. How long can I keep up with my diaries I wonder before my luck runs out should I stop now but I can't—I must go on writing or I'll go mad not being able to write down my thoughts.

Monday, 11 October 1943
Yesterday's episode is now being referred to as the 'Double Tenth'—the day the Japanese Kemp-Tai (Secret Military Police) descended on Civilian Internment Camp. They were sure they would find a spy ring, transmitters etc. with the idea that we were going to sabotage the Island of Singapore. The result—28 men were taken away and a couple of women. Even the Bishop of Singapore was included. They were taken away to be questioned and tortured I guess. We don't know exactly what is to become of them.

Everything appeared quiet. I started to write on a piece of paper about yesterday and what I thought when suddenly there were the sounds of heavy boots and voices. Hastily I got rid of the piece of paper and quickly ran outside and lay down pretending to be asleep. Up they went, their boots 'clanging' on the iron stairs, flashing their torches, then down they went. Later I heard them again going into the Carpenter's Shop and I nearly passed out in fear as I remembered that's where I was writing and what have I done with the paper—I can't remember—my mind is a blank. Oh, God! Did I drop it somewhere in my hurry to get over here? What if the Japs found it—Think, think! But I can't—I know I haven't got it with me and I can't leave here to look for it. All quiet at last—dare I go back to the Carpenter's Shop to look for it? Better not and see what happens.

Tuesday, 12 October 1943
It took me a long time to get to sleep—my mind went over and over again trying to visualise what I did when I heard those footsteps the first time. Tossed and turned—Nellie got cross with me for keeping her awake. Finally sleep came and with it a strange dream—I was woken by a young man who wore a soldier's uniform—I could not see his face but heard his voice—a strange voice and the

words he used were foreign to me but I seemed to know what he wanted me to do—go back to the Carpenter's Shop and I will find what I am looking for. I woke up very early this morning and quietly tiptoed into the Carpenter's Shop and immediately knew exactly what I had to do. Quickly I went to a pile of firewood stacked ready for our morning tea-making and instinctively I put my hand under the pile at one corner of the stack and withdrew my piece of paper—apparently I had hurriedly poked it in there when I heard the Japs coming and somehow I had forgotten what I had done with it. Strange how the subconscious works—I am glad I found it as it happened I was writing about the 'Double Tenth'—could I have been taken away and tortured on the strength of that? I don't know—the Japs are funny about certain things—the trouble is that we don't know what those 'certain things' are!

Thursday, 14 October 1943
7.30 a.m.—while we were having our showers the Nips came around to inspect us in our naked glory! Later at 11 a.m. they came around again—some of us were searched by a Chinese girl who came with them.

Friday, 15 October 1943
The Nips are on the prowl again! Have to be very careful with my notes—can't spend too much time in writing in case I get caught.

Tuesday, 19 October 1943
Since the 'Double Tenth' we've had the Nips doing their rounds at all hours of the night. Two of them entered our cell—had a good look around, picked up a couple of the school books—I tried to look unconcerned. Last night heard strange noises—sounded like tanks or heavy machinery moving.

Wednesday, 20 October 1943
Woke up by howling wind—dark clouds hid the moon. Looked like we're in for a drenching—hurriedly got up and scuttled inside then decided to stay put and enjoy the cooling wind.

Monday, 1 November 1943
Called to the Office this afternoon, worried thinking that my diaries have been discovered—was told I had to go alone with the sentry. Entered the room—there

were several of the Nipponese guards present. Was asked some questions regarding name and nationality. The Officer looked down a register and then handed me a postcard with my name on it. Addressee's name unknown but hand writing familiar. It was from Fidelis, my Godmother but she's now Mrs Remeguis A D'cruz . . .

Saturday, 6 November 1943
Roll Call 10 a.m. in the Rose Garden. No bread yesterday. This morning water off early and shortage of bubu. Have been busy with washing undertaken for M. Another cold, cold shower. Roll Call ended at around 11 a.m. Again no bread and food well below standard—something's up, for sure.

Tuesday, 9 November 1943
M's got a cold and in bed—looks pretty flushed. Took her washing out for the day. Later took washing back to her—M saw the clean hankies on top—eyes opened wide with relief and said in a low voice 'Ah, most welcomed'.

Men stopped coming—tiffin served in Rose Garden corridor—just like old times—queuing over again!

Friday, 12 November 1943
Had a late night—slept outside—moon full but watery looking. Having problem with my eyes—itchy and sore—Mrs Milne suggests I see the 'doc' tomorrow. Saw M later today who said, 'Your eyes giving you trouble? That's because you are reading and writing in the bad light. I know—I saw you' she accused me—my gaze faltered for I knew she was right.

Examined my eyes and said I've got an infection—given an eye wash and told to wear dark glasses—no reading, sewing or writing (I wonder how she expects me to while away my time).

Monday, 15 November 1943
Sister Constance had to go into hospital—seems a few more of us are having to spend time in hospital lately—our health is suffering mainly with dysentery, spates of malarial attacks and of course malnutrition. Being hungry all the time is getting beyond a joke—guess we'd eat anything that's going!

Wednesday, 17 November 1943
Having Roll Calls every Saturday now. Rained pretty heavily last night. Early morning awakened by a loud, strange droning—explanations many—some said planes, others artillery moving, etc. Went on for about ½ hour. Have been trying my hand at writing stories and verses (of sorts).

The Dream
(with apologies)

Her voice sounded sweeter and her words
Rang clearer than the songs of the birds;
Her face seemed lovelier and her ways
More loving and tender. In a few days
She changed completely and her smile
Took on a more motherly style—
Still the Mother of my dreams and yet not the same
She seemed different somehow when her children came.
There was serene happiness on their face
That marked the change that had taken place—
Through her eyes she seemed to see
All the lovely things that would be . . .

Friday, 19 November 1943
Still having treatment for my eyes. Under 21 years to get bananas and also am allowed extra bun for heavy chores every second day. Mrs Gordon in hospital again—having eye trouble. M improving—but cough not improving—looking very tired too.

Saturday, 27 November 1943
Usual Roll Call—alphabetically this time. Heard 60 new internees coming and Printer's Shop must be cleared by Tuesday. Dr Worth busy arranging for older people in Carpenter's Shop. Having supper in school room. Several people changing cells and complete blackout for tomorrow night!

Thursday, 2 December 1943
New internees not here yet—authorities said we are not prepared to receive them and huts have to be built for them. Mrs Gordon not allowed visitors. Fossy gone

back to AIII. Rumours of all kinds doing the rounds. There is also an edginess amongst the women—it doesn't seem to take much for a quarrel to start.

Monday, 6 December 1943
New arrivals! Local people—two hundred more to come—where are we going to put them I wonder. The whole place is so crowded already and tempers do fray frequently!

Wednesday, 8 December 1943
Two years since Japan dropped the bomb on Singapore—two years! Is it really two years ago—I remember so clearly that day in Cameron Highlands—Ah, Cameron Highlands . . .

Wonder how much longer before we get out of this place! Holiday for Nippon. No internees today. Mrs Gordon ill again—no visitors allowed.

Thursday, 9 December 1943
Had a really bad night—head ached and had the shivers. Some babies cry most of the night. Early morning woken with the sound of heavy rain. Steam off again so men got us our tea at 8–8.30 with the usual bubu and again at 3.30 p.m. Good news—husbands and wives allowed to meet Christmas Day.

Friday, 10 December 1943
Delightful and refreshing sleep—cool and breezy—have bed near my 'garden path' between shower and bank. The rushing water from the drain into the lower one sounds really peaceful and I am undisturbed here—reminds me—strange as it seems—of the streams up Cameron Highlands! Miss Nicholson offered me her bed while she sleeps in the treatment room and I accepted—very kind of her.

Sunday, 19 December 1943
Had another Roll Call yesterday. Thinking of what to get for Joyce's Xmas present—perhaps I could make a mattress for her—out of mine—Joyce managed to get sacking for case. Worked hard at it. Joyce wanted to help but I said 'no'. Quite pleased with the effort—produced two mattresses out of one! One of the new internees wanted to buy one of them—'Not for sale' I said as it's a Xmas present for a friend—said willing to pay $25 for it, but said 'No'. She wanted to know what am I getting

out of it. 'Friendship' I said. 'Is that all? For all that work—I am willing to pay, you know.'

'I'm sorry but her friendship means more to me than money.'

'Well, I must say, whoever she is, she is lucky to have you for a friend.'

'I don't know about that—I think I'm the lucky one to have her as a friend. She has never had a mattress and it's time she had one. Besides, I can't sell a Xmas present, can I?'

She smiled—'I understand'.

Proudly I carried the two mattresses and went into the schoolroom in search of Joyce. There she was and I gave it to her—there was astonishment on her face— 'For me? Oh, Sheila, you are a treasure! Thank you so much. My—it's nice and soft' as she hugged it to herself.

Tuesday, 21 December 1943

Another batch of new arrivals—all from upcountry. After tea Mrs Fincher called for the Heavy Fatigue to go to the Nips' office to pick up Xmas gifts from POW— heard that the POWs gave $800 to Lady Thomas as a gift to the Camp. Hive of activity all round—getting ready for Xmas.

Saturday, 25 December 1943

Xmas Day—again! Our second Xmas in Changi Gaol and we thought we'd be out of here before this—who said that? Went to Mass. After breakfast helped to distribute all the presents. Received a little autograph book from M. Had given her a pair of cami-knicks that I had made and note which I wrote as follows:–

'All that you wish yourself today, I wish you and please accept this gift as a mother would because I know exactly how you feel about it. I do not want you to think that you ought to do something in return, for if you do, it is I who will be under an obligation, not you. Please do not thank me. The pleasure of doing this for you is all the thanks I allow myself. Besides, what I really want is not easy to obtain. So I am quite content and thankful for small mercies that come to brighten my way. It is a year today since I have known you personally and I thank you for giving me something I will cherish all my life—meaning yourself and the memory of you after this—thank you for all that you have done for me— for your patient care—your gentle reproof and sound advice—for your sympathy and discretion—for listening to me and above all for being what you are to me— my Dream Mother, my Inspiration. Thank you "Mother" is all that I can say for these little things that mean so much to me. God bless you and all those you love and others who love you. May today be for you as happy as it can possibly be in here. I pray, also, that for you, the next Xmas will find you in the midst of your loved ones.'

Shared a tin of chicken curry at tiffin. Later got dressed for our relatives' meeting in the Rose Garden. Saw Dad who is looking very thin and suddenly very old. There were tears in his eyes as he hugged me and I wished to God that we'll leave this place soon for his sake as I can see that he is slowly fading away.

Children's party at 6 p.m. At 5 p.m. stationed myself at the schoolroom door, keeping the children from entering. Kept pretty busy. An officer and two sentries accompanied the boys across the courtyard.

Father Xmas (Mrs Kennard again) also received a present—and was surprised! Had sweets as well.

Together with Phyliss, we went to the hospital to wish the patients a Happy Xmas. Saw Mrs Cornelius—surprised and regardless of rules went to speak to her. Said she's just a little tired and needed a rest. Told her she'd been working too hard . . .

Then saw Mrs Gordon, gently touched her hand so as not to frighten her and quietly wished her a happy Xmas. She was surprised and with her dark glasses she couldn't see who it was—then, 'Oh, it's you, my dear' when she recognised my voice. 'It's nice to see you, Sheila' and laughed. Asked how she was—'Much better and going to the San, later.' She looked so thin and somehow so sad and then I knew the reason for her sadness—'I received bad news today—my youngest nephew, my sister's child, is dead. He was killed—died of wounds.'

'I am sorry' and held her hand tight.

The night sister came over and said it was time to leave.

Monday, 27 December 1943

Feeling off colour today. A door banged—someone yelled excitedly. 'Listen—a bomb!' Then Mrs K came in and said quite seriously, 'Singapore is up in flames!' A babble of voices—'Yes, yes! The Americans have dropped bombs just now.'

Could it be true? Guess we wanted to believe that it's true. Rumours of repatriation again going around. More internees came in from KL—also a nun from Malacca Convent! Blackout all of a sudden—poor Miss Martin in the middle of having a bath and in the confusion kicked the bucket of water. Her cell mate wasn't very impressed with the 'wet' mess! Things got a bit heated between the two women— then the lights came on and there wasn't that much of a mess after all!

Friday, 31 December 1943

Roll Call today. Had camp cleaned yesterday for the inspection—then had no water

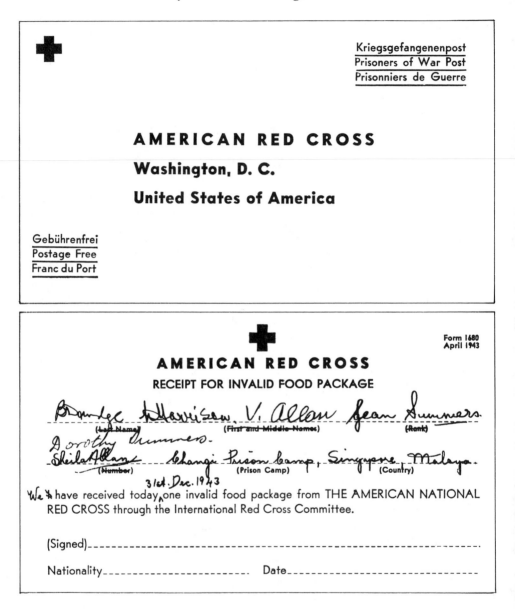

yesterday evening! Have been making calendars for M, Cornelius, Worth and Smith and a bookmark for Stiffy White.

Red Cross parcels given out today—one parcel between 6 people—fell on me to collect it for our group.

Items included—1 tin prunes; 1 tin powdered milk; 1 packet cheese; 2 bars chocolate; 1 packet sugar; 2 bars soap; 8 packets vegetable protein soups; 2 tins coffee; 10 packets cigarettes (for the smokers); 1 tin salmon; 3 tins (tiny) butter; 3 small tins corned pork; 1 tin Premium; 1 small tin grape jam; 2 tins chopped ham and eggs; 1 tin Bovril cornbeef; 1 tin Rosemill Pate. What a lovely New Year's present!

Helped Miss MacDonald with free issue of coconut oil by ticking names off the list. Saw Mrs Cornelius again—not looking so well. Barbara Smith pleased with the calendar. Stiffy White delighted with her bookmark.

Afternoon Mrs Gregory told me to see Dr Worth—guessed it's about Dad—I was right but Dr Worth said not to worry too much—Dad suffering from high blood pressure and under observation. Will keep me informed of his progress. Poor Dad—what next?

1944

Saturday, 1 January 1944

Coffee party till 12.30 p.m. Greeted the New Year with singing and dancing and a few tears flowing freely from us all. Wonder what is in store for us in 1944—freedom?

Oh, God, deliver us from all this soon, soon. After a lot of hugging and wishing we went off to our respective resting places. I was too keyed up to go to sleep—just sat on the steps looking out at the stars, thinking my own thoughts.

Friday, 14 January 1944

Joyce's birthday and she's 21! I wonder if I'll have my 21st birthday here too! But that's 2 years away—surely we'll be out of here then or will we? Had a quiet birthday treat for Joyce. Later I sat with Pauline, Xenia and Kyra and we started talking about spiders, fairies and our war experiences. Xenia spoke of the two men who were under a truck that caught fire—they were covered in oil and they implored their mates to shoot them before the Japs could get to them. After, saw some of the prisoners with their hands bored and screwed together—how dreadful!

Then I told them what I had seen the day after we surrendered—a dying Chinese woman lying on the road with her tummy gashed open and her baby lying not far away with its head almost severed from its body—both of them just alive!

I think the bombing did that. Later I witnessed a Jap sentry plunge his sword into a baby's tummy to kill it and he had a smile on his face! It was horrible! I couldn't help shivering, remembering that look on the man's face—as if he was enjoying what he was doing to that baby. Horrible vision to have before my eyes—can I ever forget—can I? Will I?

We sat in silence for a while. Then Xenia spoke. 'You know, Sheila, I don't know what to do or think. If only Ray is here or even my brother.'

'Do you love Ray? Do you know where he is?'

'I don't know where he is and I don't know if I love him. I thought I did. I was very unhappy at home and I was lonely and I guess he was lonely too. Now I miss him sometimes and at other times I have no feelings. When all this is over and if I don't see him again I don't think I'd mind. Maybe he's changed too.'

'What about the one next door?'

'I don't know about him though I'm told he's crazy about me.'

'Tell me, Xenia, do you believe in love and marriage?'

'Sure I do. I don't think I can marry a man I don't love. What about you, Sheila?'

'I don't think I will marry—seen too many marriages break up.'

'I know and I feel so depressed—sometimes I want to end it all.'

'Don't say that. There's life ahead of you. It's being in here that's making you and me feel so down in the dumps. This nightmare must end one day—I only wish that day comes soon. Come on, Xenia, let's try and get some sleep—you know, what time it is? 2.30 in the morning!'

Thursday, 20 January 1944

Had dancing last night from 6.30 to 7.30 p.m. and to be on every Thursday. Poor Mrs F has been heard singing lustily in her cell—quite weird, I believe and someone suggested that she's going 'batty'!

Sunday, 23 January 1944

We now have a new team of Officers—Women's Representatives—Mrs Chowns; Deputy—Miss MacDonald; Camp Superintendent—Mrs Jennings; Deputy—Miss Haggarty; Fatigue officer—Mrs Toussaint.

Orders—no smoking after 10 p.m.—a blow for the heavy smokers!

Heard from Maureen that five men are suffering from diabetes and insulin will last either end of the month or next! The 'fairies' (nickname for the Nips because of their frequent 'flitting' rounds!!!) been asked for insulin supplies—no supplies yet.

Wednesday, 26 January 1944

Feeling sick today—off food and aching all over. Had to see the Doc to get permission to be off work tomorrow and instead got carted to hospital—malaria again!

Sunday, 13 February 1944

Came out of hospital yesterday—ended up with a very bad cough. Chest sore from constant coughing. Mum worried in case it's TB as there have been a couple of cases about. Weight loss—steady—now down to less than 7 stone!

Heard Miss Harnett had a stroke—account given by Mary M: Miss Harnett's sister heard her cry out for help and found her on the floor. Mary Scott and Dr

Worth arrived to take charge. A priest was called as Miss H remained unconscious this morning.

Explosion yesterday evening. Diet—only rice and soup with bubu this morning and evening—don't feel like eating much yet.

Tuesday, 15 February 1944

Xenia taken by the Nips to office last night—locked up and Mrs Chown slept in the office. Guess someone put her in? Her cell was raided today as well as her boyfriend's. Nothing was found.

Apparently a letter was sent to Mr B (from a 'white person'—Mr B's words!) accusing them of writing letters. Now told if caught 'a week's solitary confinement; if caught with letter—6 months and if letter contains news of war, your head would be off—also for rules broken in Camp, no matter how small will not go unpunished. Now we know what to expect!

Sunday, 20 February 1944

Teaching Jeannie embroidery. Jews moved to huts and rice store. Fossy and Mrs Mul had an argument about cotton thread for men's mending articles but things got sorted out in the end. Asked Fossy if rumour about the Japs asking M to resign from office true—only said that the Japs thought M is not well enough for the job!

Wednesday, 23 February 1944

Have been taking food to Mrs Harrison and Davidge—both not well. Mrs Broadbent is ill with fever and I have been taking food to her too.

Been raining for some days now. Food bad—buns and soup. Mornings and evenings bubu—no rice—only beans, peanuts, sago flour and water. Many of us are suffering from the 'Trots'.

Monday we had (wonder of wonders!) fish at 9 p.m. in the schoolroom—there were shouts of 'fish, fish' and before you could say 'Jack Robinson' the schoolroom was swarming with screaming jostling females! Just like a fish market—the noise was! Suddenly the lights went out—pandemonium!!! Then the lights came on again—you'd swear someone was playing a game with us.

'How come everybody's getting such a small piece?'

'How small? Show me!'

'Mine is smaller than yours' and so it goes on, everybody talking at the same time—actually it was only a morsel! It smelt like fish but tasted like nothing. 'Hope it's fresh' crossed my mind but what the heck it was food after all!

Friday, 25 February 1944

Silence from 12 to 12.30 p.m. for siren practice. Barbara and I talking about marriage now that Irene and Diana are engaged—wonder if it is possible to have a wedding in here—not likely!!! Can you just imagine how many marriages there would be if weddings were allowed?

Someone did a mess in front of M's cell last night and those sleeping near were practically sick all night with the smell. M had to clean it all up with the help of Marie Robinson and Mrs Mather.

Mrs Shelton Palmer had a heart attack. Heard that Mrs B wrote letter to the 'Fairies' complaining that some had second servings of food and she was not allowed to have any and so she now refuses to have her own ration. The Kitchen staff was called before 'B'—they explained that she was a little off her head—always thinking that she was being poisoned by us—showed him her ration saying that they give her a little more than anyone else. Asked how some got 'seconds' and others not—he was told that turns were taken. Mrs B had had hers the other day and of course she's not entitled until her turn comes. So 'B' said 'What is she complaining about? If that is her ration and she won't take it, let her starve. She's fat enough. Even I have lost weight since I've come here as the diet is so poor. Let her go without it.'

Let's hope that's the end of that—no more letters from Mrs B.

Saturday, 26 February 1944

Last night 'B' came round—smelt of drink—very friendly and chattered with a few of us. I was going to Mrs Harrison's cell with some rice and spinach and asked her if she wanted any. 'B' came in—'All young people' and looked at the food. 'Is your dinner?'

'Yes,' I replied.

'You eat it now?'

'Yes.'

'Good. Do not waste anything now. Food hard to get.'

'Oh, no' I said. 'I'm too hungry to throw any food away.'

Nodded his head—'Very hungry. No food to waste.' Looked behind the door. 'What's that?' as he lifted the teacosy. 'You all married?'

'Yes' came the answer.

'You too?' incredulously of Mum who nodded. 'You look too young' he said. Turned to me, 'You too?'

'No'

'Ah!' was all he said. Asked if we wanted to see our husbands.

'We would like to' answered Mrs Harrison.

'Yes! Perhaps once a month or maybe once a week, yes?' we all nodded our heads. 'But there are men with no wives and women no husbands—so if we allow you to meet—it is not nice—they not like and be jealous.'

'Yes, that can be true, too' we said.

He seemed puzzled at this reply. Turning to me, 'You have husband.'

'My father is here in the Men's Camp.'

'Maybe sweetheart, yes?'

'No.'

'Ah! plenty men in Camp.'

'Yes, but we don't get a chance to see them.'

'You like to try' he persisted.

'But we can't see them,' I answered warily as I became suspicious.

'What you do all day?' He asked watching me.

'Work, read, play, school'—(a slip there)

'School! No school'

'I mean not real school—just talking about friends and telling stories to the children.'

'I see. Just now what you talk about—love stories, maybe?' We smiled. After another look around—'Okay—goodnight' and left us to wonder what was in his mind. He wasn't that drunk as he took a good look around the cell, hoping I suppose to see if he could find anything unusual or perhaps he thought we were up to something being closeted in a group! He even stopped to ask Xenia as he went out if she was still sending kisses to her boyfriend. Looks like we all have to be very careful from now on.

Sunday, 27 February 1944

Water off again last night and all day today. Camp stinks terribly. 'B' in bad mood today. Food ration cut to ½. Had a spot of rain and we rushed to catch the heaven-sent water but it lasted only a few seconds. Situation pretty desperate. When the water came on there was such a rush to get to the water, the cisterns had no chance to fill up. The water kept going off and on at ½ hourly intervals until a quarter to 9 p.m. Managed to get a shower late and managed to wash my hair (at last!).

The office shifted to Red Cross Hut. Mrs Shelton Palmer much better today.

Wednesday, 1 March 1944

Monday and Tuesday ¼ ration of rice. Today no buns and ½ ration of rice. Hunger pains! Filling up with water. Legs swelling and what a 'pot' belly I am developing!

Red Cross Hut opens today in one of the E huts. Yesterday evening had an informal Children's Exhibition in the schoolroom. Had surprise for supper—no bubu but a new kind of bun—sweet potato! Had our pay too! ($5).

Saturday, 4 March 1944

Menu for today—breakfast as usual. Tiffin—soup and coffee, no rice. Supper—fish paste and Red Palm Oil Cake—no bubu.

Yesterday—no rice. Food seems to be getting less but ration of papayas and pineapples given out. Can't understand shortage of rice when fruit is being brought in.

Rumours going around again—many think this is going to be an eventful month and could be out before Xmas. 'Hope springs eternal!'

Sunday, 12 March 1944

Roll Call—rumour of Armistice being signed and could be announced at Roll Call! Two nights ago drone of planes woke the Camp. There was a buzz of excitement as we tried to figure out what all this meant.

Maternity cases to be in Camp from now on. Mrs Flower appears to be getting worse. Found her singing 'There was an old woman who lived in a shoe. She had no children but she knew what to do. Ha, ha, ha!' Found a hammer and threw it at one of the children—fortunately her aim wasn't too good and no one was hurt. Came towards me, still singing in a high pitch voice. Looked at me for what seemed like a long time. Prodded me with a finger and asked 'Am I mad?'

'Of course not' I said.

'Do you think I am mad?'

'Why should I? You are no more mad than I am and I don't think I am mad. Do you think I am mad?' I asked her.

'No-oo-oo' she replied. Picked up a cushion—'Feel this cushion—it's heavy, don't you think?'

'Yes, it feels heavy' I told her.

'I can knock you out with it, can't I?'

'Yes, I guess you can but you won't, will you?'

'No-oo-oo' she shook her head. Looks like a 'cat and mouse' game this. She laughed—'You such a dear little thing and you are my friend, my friend. How about a kiss then' and she turned her cheek towards me. Gave her a peck and gently guided her towards the hospital. Sister took over and asked her 'How are you, Mrs Flower?'

'I'm very ill, thank you' she replied. I feel we all are going to be pretty sick before long.

Wednesday, 15 March 1944
General inspection at 1 p.m. Lunch at 12.30 p.m. Offered to help wash corridors. These inspections are getting to be a nuisance—seems as if the Nips are trying to catch us doing something we are not supposed to be doing. Only have two more exercise books to write my diary in—writing has been getting smaller and smaller. Soon the ink will run out and I'll have to resort to writing in pencil.

Sunday, 19 March 1944
Fossy's birthday (58). Yesterday M informed that Dad's in hospital again but not to worry—some minor illness! Having eye trouble had application of silver nitrate—pretty painful. Barbara better again. Saw Mrs Gordon—improving. Mrs Shelton Palmer—no change. Orr and Redfern—critical condition.

Tuesday, 21 March 1944
Heard the following related—'How dare you suggest that woman to be my cell mate' and a lot more—reason Mrs C had either to double up or go to the Carpenter's Shop. She chose the latter.
Children's Fancy Dress Parade today in the Rose Garden at 6.30 p.m. There were free issues of sweets, biscuits and peanut toffee according to the draws:-
(1) If draw toffee, get ½ packet of sweets
(2) If draw sweets, get ½ packet of toffee
(3) If biscuits, get 6 ozs of biscuits.
By order of the powers-that-be—the flower gardens to be converted into vegetable gardens. Seed and cuttings will be provided.
Saw the parade—excellent and several of the children contributed an item.
It was great seeing them enjoying themselves—especially Hugh Davidson and Eileen Harris. Results of the prize-winners will be known later. Looked after Janice while her mother took care of Billy who was feeling off colour.
Told bean bun if taken in excess has a 'maddening' effect so we are getting salt fish paste to counter act the 'madness!'—seems strange. Accounts of weird goings on like Mrs Lopez believing that there is someone sitting on top of our floor every night in the dark and that one night she went into her cell and she was positive that there was someone else sitting in the dark. Ghosts???

Thursday, 23 March 1944
Papayas given out today. Mrs Gordon looking more like herself. Mrs Macleod gone into hospital—poor woman—she's really very bitter at losing her husband

I started training as a nurse in 1946 at the Queen Victoria Memorial Hospital. This is my graduation photo, 1949. (Original print)

Return to Changi Prison, 16 February 1992. The courtyard and the Men's Camp are in the background. (© Examiner Newspaper Pty Ltd)

Sime Road Camp, 17 February 1992.

and blamed the 'fairies' for having killed him by not allowing her to nurse him as she felt she could have saved him by nursing him herself. Saw her in hospital and all I could do was to let her cry!

Saturday, 25 March 1944

Free issue of Gula Batu—½ lb (Changi) Peanut Toffee, sweets and biscuits have also come in. Mail from 'Home' has arrived and there is a newspaper for all to read in the schoolroom from 9.30 a.m. to 12.30 p.m. and from 4.30 p.m. to 5.30 p.m.

Last night was looking after Janice in the Printer's Shop—heard a loud 'thud' and a child cried out and heard that Mrs Pereria had fallen. Two floor walkers carried her out and I offered to fetch M. Dared not leave Janice by herself so took her with me. Told Sister on duty to tell M. Walked back with her and explained what had happened. Wanted to know if she had fainted—all I knew was that she fell—maybe she slipped with her child.

'Is this Janice? She's a lovely child, isn't she and you kept us amused in hospital, didn't you, Janice?' She spoke softly. Janice was very quiet.

Afternoon while resting Sheila Summers woke me up with the news that Mrs Bloom and Dr Williams have returned—also Mr Stevens, M and Dr Worth were called and the two women were put in hospital. Wonderful to have them back with us again—wonder if I will ever know what happened to them while outside— guess they must have had a terrible time judging by their physical appearance. Mrs Bloom looks really ill. Mrs Orr dying—a priest was in attendance.

Seven men were also returned to the Camp—Hugh Fraser, Adrian Clarke, Norman Coulson, Stanley, John Long (shot)—7 dead and 16 more to go. Mrs Orr died this morning. Sad day all round.

Saturday, 1 April 1944

April Fool's Day—not a fool today! 10 oz of Gula Batu today. Met M on the stairs: 'Oh, Sheila, is it true that you found a dead rat in your spinach?' I stared at her. 'Where did you get that story from?' I asked.

'Well, someone said that you found something sticking out from the spinach. Thinking it was a piece of stalk, you pulled it out and found it was a rat's tail.'

I laughed out loud—'I think you've been had—it's April Fool's Day!'

Some talk about a surprise tomorrow. Heard there's a snake in the vicinity.

Also some thieving going on in the Printer's Shop—midnight prowlers going through people's things. Most unpleasant thought. I can see that we're going to have to be very watchful.

Sunday, 2 April 1944
Choir practice for Easter. Evening heard Mrs Nixon taken away. Fossy very upset and also expects to be called by the Nips. Freddy Bloom looking more like her old self. Heard M, Dr Robinson, Mrs Chowns, Meir, Lady Thomas and Lady Heath had to answer questions on Camp life. Wonder what's going on in the Nips' minds—trying to set a trap, I think.

Friday, 7 April 1944
Good Friday. Had hot steam on from 10 a.m. to 1 p.m. Breakfast—mashed corn. Way of the Cross from 10.30 a.m. to 11.15 a.m. During service—rained pretty heavily. Chairs and tables wet but rain stopped about 11.30 a.m. and the men started to come in. Dad was among the first group—very thin but looks reasonably well. Told Dad about decision to do Senior Certificate exam.

Heard from Fossy that Adrian Clarke and Buchannan are dead, believed killed!

Freddy says men marvellous especially Clarke—full of courage—thinks Mrs Nixon might be treated more leniently—let's hope so. It makes me a little, no, a lot nervous about my diary—I feel the time has come for me to ease up a bit besides how am I going to continue if I run out of paper—I like to keep on writing. I must keep on writing—I can't stop now.

Saturday, 8 April 1944
Dad's birthday—55 today—gave him hankies that I had made. Told him that I have decided to take up nursing when we get out of here.

Men had a concert in their yard—very pleasant listening. More rumours of repatriation. Free issue of toffee, sweets and biscuits, also papayas. Had 'coffee elevenses' with Mrs Bryant.

Saturday, 15 April 1944
First baby girl born in Changi this afternoon—the Printers' floor walker collected about $70 as a surprise for the new mother and baby. Went in early this morning—baby weighs about 5 lbs. Sugar ration today. Wonder if a name has been chosen for the baby.

Friday, 21 April 1944
Janice not well. Fossy has a bad throat and confined to bed. Found out that other children under father's nationality and mine is No. 1 Eurasian—going to find out

about it but Mrs Brooks saved me the trouble—said would include my name under 'Aust'.

Inspection cancelled because of heavy rain. Food very scarce—urgent need for food containing Vitamin B; beans, nuts, peas and rice polishings.

For whom it may concern (present and future)
The following letter has been received from a member of this Camp. It voices the feelings of many—'Long internment seems to have exhausted many people's resources in the clothing line and the scantiest of Scanties, and the Flimsiest of Panties, have been evolved to meet the needs of the moment and to stave as long as possible the day when Changi of necessity becomes a Nudist Colony. Until that evil day arrives could it be suggested that now sentries are in the Camp at all hours and we have no privacy, the more frail of undergarments should be discreetly veiled when doing chores such as ironing and only worn without covering when inside one's cell. We have no orders from the Nipponese as to what we should or should not wear 'below the waist' but they did mention 'Suntops as being inadequate'.

Saturday, 22 April 1944
Had inspection today—only Major General Saito speaking—the literal translation of his speech by 'Bamba'—

Major wants to speak about yesterday. It was off because of the terrible rain so change it for this morning. Ladies, children may I introduce the new Commandant of this Camp. At present the Nipponese forces are in Burma and have invaded India across the border and have reached a point near Impah. The war in the Pacific is being waged with great intensity. USA warships and submarines as well as aircraft are attacking Jap (or Nip occupied territory) day and night without cessation.

But Japan is strong and cannot be defeated and will continue to fight. All Japanese men and women and children are determined to give their utmost in the cause of this war. When the war will finish no one knows but when it ends Jap and Br and USA will arrange Ex ships and you will go back to your countries, to your families and friends. At that time you will wish to return in ex. health. Therefore take care of yourselves and this will be a fine gift to your wives, children, sisters and other relatives. I will do my very best regarding food and supplies but you must appreciate the difficulties of the present situation.

(Note:– In the front courtyard Major General Saito used the expression 'Exchange boat next trip' but said he knew nothing of any arrangements for any move from this Camp. This translation is issued from the Office of the Men's Representative and not from the Nip Authorities). After this Mrs Byrne had an interview with Tominaga about identity tabs—very nice and said will look into it. Evening the following written on the notice board:– 'For general information—Mr Miamoto called me this evening to explain to me that the principal objective of the General's visit was to point out the difficulties of looking after us properly, shortage of supplies and materials and the difficult war situation. Also that if we would put up with our troubles for a little while longer—say a month or less—we should get some very good news and we should be "Banyak, banyak baik" (very, very good) and that everyone including Miamato himself would be very happy. He said he could not reveal the nature of the good news but that I was at liberty to tell everyone of his conversation with me' (signed Dr Elyn Evans – Men's Representative). The whole Camp started talking—opinions:- 1. . . . Red Cross ships; repatriation or peace—I—on the level—instead of elation—suspicious and wondering.

Sunday, 23 April 1944
Still rumours going around—one of the men—asked one of the sentries if Red Cross Ships—reply—better than that. Fossy gone to San for a few days. New moon—several people bowed to it!

Tuesday, 25 April 1944
Tonsillitis! Rumours and more rumours. Talk about going away—where?—just somewhere. When?—who knows.

Baby boy born tonight—mother said her previous delivery was forceps so all was in readiness—not needed, baby arrived safely. Baby named Desmond Anthony Dleiman—6½ lbs.

Baby girl born last week—named Geraldine April Hawley. No news of Mrs Nixon.

Great excitement! On noticeboard—within a few days going to be moved to another Camp—Sime Road, Bukit Timah—possessions arranged for transfer—Collinge Committee in charge of this—date not known but will be informed from time to time.

Saturday, 29 April 1944
Emperor's birthday—meeting from 11 a.m. to 12 noon—a surprise indeed. Jap showering sweets—scramble from children! 3 men died and one committed suicide—that's 2 in the Men's. Heard Australian and other soldiers taking our place and we theirs—date still uncertain—rumour of repatriation again.

Sunday, 30 April 1944
Men going tomorrow (1,350) a batch of 450 in 15 lorries—30 in each—with bedding and an attache case or small handbags. We—moving floor by floor—AV

first. Feeling down and out. Heard 30 to a hut. Aussies taking our place here. Seems 2 Red Cross ships arrived today bringing Miamato's wife—no wonder it's 'Banyak, banyak baik' for him. Later heard was only rumours.

Monday, 1 May 1944

News—not moving till Monday 8th. M and Mrs Chowns went to see new camp. All packed except few essentials—Nips not to be trusted—could change their minds to an earlier date. Now told could be 70 to a hut for about 10–20 days—have to do own cooking. Hospital staff and workers can get accommodation near hospital. Heard Susuki angry for removing us but military orders—also Miamoto surprised we take this as the 'Banyak, banyak baik' news. Seems some girls going over on roof of schoolroom to meet men—if caught we'll all be in trouble.

Thursday, 4 May 1944

All furniture, planks, boxes, chairs, tables and non-essential things taken down yesterday evening—heavy stuff for men's fatigue today—things moving today. Lights allowed until 11.30 p.m. and again on at 6.30 a.m. and breakfast at 7.30 a.m. Been busy helping to pack—quite a hive of activity!

Saturday, 6 May 1944

What a night! 'F' was up to her old tricks again—disturbing the peace with her singing and going on about wanting to sleep outside. It was raining outside and 'F' took her bed out. Mrs W tried to stop her from going to bed out there and there was an argument. Joyce and I tried to help Mrs W to quieten Mrs F but no go—so went to get M. 'F' refused to get inside so M and Mrs W carried her in while Joyce and I carried the bed. All quiet so I settled down to sleep but not for long—'F' burst into song. M came out with a tablet for her—took it and then spat it out and was going to take the glass but M was too quick and got the glass out of harm's way. 'F' began to cry saying she wanted to sleep outside and watch the moon and the like—lot of talk. M spoke to Mrs W who called me to help take bed out—did so—M made her get in—turned to her—'I will get into bed but I won't sleep, you know'. M sat with her—got Trudie's shirt for her—later Mrs W brought a blanket for her—sat long time—when got up 'F' started to hum—sat down again—finally left and sat some yards away to watch—'F' gesticulating in the air—at last all quiet—had gone to sleep—so I closed eyes—this morning woke early but breakfast as usual. Saw M who thanked me for helping her. News—moving this afternoon—all adults—families next day. Saw Dutch troops coming in—very cheerful and seeing us—put 'thumbs' up.

Sunday, 7 May 1944   **Sime Road Camp**

New Camp! Left Changi Prison about ½ past 2 this afternoon—in 7 lorries—men helped with luggage—gave hot tea to drink. A lovely, cool ride but not long enough. Fresh air—green, green everywhere—everything looks so normal! Volunteers needed for tin shed—Hut 16—separated from Mum—with Aunty Maude. Men ready to help us when we arrived. A bit of shifting about—first to go to the tin shed then told to go to the 'Flying Dutchman Hut' (must be the name the POWs gave it when here.)

Got turfed out of that to go to Hut 16. Later told to go to Hut 14, then back to the Flying Dutchman, again to Hut 12—talk about moves on the chessboard!

Finally settled in Hut 5 but for the night! Evening told to be ready to move to Hut 16 in the morning.

Monday, 8 May 1944

Spent all day sorting luggage and personal belongings.

13 in our Hut—congested—roof leaks—mozzies very bad. The rest of Changi arrived today. Lots of names written on the walls of the Hut—Mrs Jean White's husband died 5 months ago—there were many other names of the POWs who died written down.

Men's Camp (temporarily) next door. The Nips had theirs above us. The 'lavs' are not too bad and there's water to drink. The gardens look neglected but guess we'll be put to work on them. Queuing for food on the road—food being brought in from the Men's Camp.

Tuesday, 9 May 1944

Slept outside—too cramped inside the Hut. Children starting to settle down. Spent most of the day cleaning wash-house and 'lavies' with 3 others—made sure that no one reserves private bathrooms and 'lavie'—moving to another Hut—Hut 1 (guard) on hillside—near hospital and road.

Volunteered for VAD at Hospital as well as work in gardens. All the Huts are overcrowded.

Saturday, 13 May 1944

At last moved (officially) to Hut 1—it's smaller than the others but it has a verandah and I've claimed a space there. Hope there won't be too much windy, wet weather—I could get a bit wet but at least I won't be disturbed by too many people and I'll be able to write without too many questions being asked. I think I shall sleep well tonight.

Sunday, 14 May 1944

Slept well last night. All day today cleared lalang [long grass] around our Hut—hard work and got some blisters on my hands. Ration of sugar given out with cheroots and cigarettes. Doing office running with messages—enjoying the freedom of being able to move around. It is good to be out in the fresh air—seeing the trees and the grass—so, so different to being cooped up within 4 walls. To be free, oh to be really free—I pray that day is not too far away.

Tuesday, 16 May 1944

Permission granted for men and women to meet daily (twice) letters are allowed—to anyone you like! But warning regarding contents. Annie is Camp Postman and I'm her assistant. Issue of Gula Batu 2 ozs for 35 cents.

Fossy had a fall and is in hospital. Heard Mrs Nixon in bad way—living in YWCA. Have been gardening—planting sweet potatoes—very sunburnt—in fact a lot of us are that way. My garden plot has chillies, tapioca, a clump of lemon grass, wild cat's whiskers and pergaga herbs—all doing well, watered by the May showers. Killed a baby snake this afternoon behind our Hut with my chunkul [mattock].

Wednesday, 17 May 1944

Roll Call 10 a.m.—A block to line up in front of Flying Dutchman and E block in front of Hut 14 and 12. Our library hours 4–5 p.m. in Hut 10. Problem with sandflies—have come out in red, itchy blotches! Outside showers being built with permission to use some of the kajang [fence].

Sunday, 21 May 1944

An incident involving one of the women with a Sikh guard—he was recognised and reported to our office and the authorities—result—woman and Sikh were slapped across their faces and told if it happened again will be put in solitary away from the Camp.

Now Sikh guards no longer posted at the gate. Having an outbreak of malaria in the Men's Camp.

Parcels allowed between Camps. Rained all day—miserable—all cooped up in the Huts.

Tuesday, 23 May 1944

Ghosts! Yes, ghosts in Hut 11, so I'm told. They make their presence felt about

10 or 11 p.m., throwing things about. Some think it is a monkey. 'J' thinks they are restless spirits. Consequently I slept very little last night!

Thursday, 25 May 1944

Mrs J. White visited husband's grave. Today Mrs R attended husband's funeral. He died last night in Miyako Hospital—supposed to be coming back to Camp. Sad to think he was not able to see his son who is now at the talking stage.

Friday, 26 May 1944

Despatched letter to 'Shakespeare' [Carl Gibson-Hill] in Dad's letter. Nearly poisoned myself today—ate wild figs—took too much—was sick about five times—felt rotten—never again! Jo offered me some more—refused—others ate but only a few with no effect. Jo took a lot but she is all right—I just happened to be the unfortunate one. Evening received letter from Dad saying he knew not Shakespeare—disapprove of the separation and to be careful of name—replied not to worry about that as I'm still a home-bird—internment has not changed me. Annie sick.

Saturday, 27 May 1944

Deputised for Annie—Red Cross letters—200 came in—enjoyed delivering them—faces joyful and sad. Confession today and church tomorrow. Hear getting bun every day—new serving utensil—quite neat and dainty. Music allowed on Wednesday and Saturday from 5–8. Jo received two chicks from Pin. She made a smart fowl-run. Visited Joyce and got a glimpse of Shakespeare—very thin. Mrs Gordon's birthday—wished her.

Tuesday, 30 May 1944

Two lovely sunny days—gorgeous sunrise and sunset. Heard news and funny doings—list of names of people in Pad. Hockenhull taken away from Camp today. Dad doesn't know Shakespeare—wrote to latter—address unknown—to see Dad if he can—hope that will work. Annie going to hospital this evening—dysentery—so am carrying on with her work—a lot of walking—makes me hungry too—like it immensely. Many sick—either dysentery or malaria. Still sleeping out. Every night about ¼ past nine—hot water for Aunty Maud from hospital—at least between 18–20 walks altogether from morning to night. Asked Dr Williams if she could start me on in nursing—quite willing so asked if there couldn't be a class for 4 as I know 3 others are keen to take up nursing—pleased to do so—1st lesson today from 6–7 p.m.—Jean Hanson—18 (age); Cecilia Lloyd Owen—16; Mary Mark—19. Next Tuesday Miss Simmons to take us in practical work. Warning given about October investigation—to be careful not to break rules—less women to be in Office—about 3.

Wednesday, 31 May 1944

No letters—Office being shifted—going to be photographed tomorrow—at Flying Dutchman while band plays from 2.00–3.00 p.m. Wanted 40 married couples with children to be photographed with husbands in Men's Camp about 20. Mum wants—groups in Men's Camp as follows—

(a) Men's Hospital
(b) At the water tank
(c) 50 gardeners
(d) 50 internees and 5 padres in Church
(e) Men's Representative (Dr Evans). Women's Representative (Mrs Chowns) and Dr Davidson receiving 'Red Cross' mail from Tominaga.

Went round with paper—on my feet from 2–5 p.m. Tired out—silly questions too. Morning while waiting for letters, two office runners wanted to know my surname—'a boy wants to know'.

'Who?'

'Jerry Howell.'

'Why?'

'He just wants to know because he sees you every day going to the office.'

'Do either of you know my name?' Heads shook. 'That's fine. I don't tell strangers my name. You can tell him that.'

'Then I'll ask my sister' said Bryant Taylor and they vanished.

Thursday, 1 June 1944

Mrs Jackson and Mrs Redfern died yesterday—attended the services at 12 and 2—very heart-rending spectacle—many cried. Left before it was over to see Dad—music had already started. Lovely view—glad put name down—Dad looking well and had a lot to say—said Shakespeare seeked him out—was disappointed because thought letter from wife and daughter—am sorry and must write and tell him so—Dad likes him and said 'A very charming man, indeed'.

Pictures taken—men playing bridge—children picking fruit and a lot of other bluffs! Heard that Mrs Ruth's husband was buried with six others in the same spot—mixed race. Heard from Dad that many of the volunteers we knew were either dead, missing or wounded. Annie out of hospital. Fried rice for supper.

Saturday, 3 June 1944
Received letter from Shakespeare . . .

Showed the address—'Miss Sheila Allan, Hut 1, Women's Camp. From Dr C.A. Gibson-Hill—Hut 40, Men's Camp' to the other party—Incredulous and so won bet [that I wouldn't write to him]—packet of cheroots—wonder if I should send to him. Aunty Maud teasing me but paying no attention—somehow feel relieved that he is married. Joyce is teased about Murphy—C/o kitchen for Women's Camp, Huts 16, 18 and Hospital.

Had fresh fish for supper. Rumour going to meet—when? Saw letter to Joan Marks from 'Modder'—my old lover??? Confession—perhaps every Saturday.

Sunday, 4 June 1944
Helped to shift Mrs Jackson's things to Office and Mrs Dowland's to Hut 16—heard meeting at ½ past 11 a.m. Went over to Men's Camp under shady trees—lovely and cool—wide spaces—saw Dad at his hut but did not come—too busy—Mum annoyed—stayed till the end—saw some sights—saw 'Modder' with the Marks' girls—what fun!—very thin and hardly recognisable now—could see Huts 101–105 clearly—'Mother' sat not far away—a woman fainted and was carried back—pictures were taken—children allowed to climb and pick fruit—several husbands and wives did not come. Caught Mrs Howell's son watching me several times as my eyes roved all over the place to observe the others—a good hour—was very pleasant surprise—wonder every Sunday.

Yesterday evening music from the Men's Camp—was not up to mark—last week's was better playing—saw Dad but he went away soon. Spoke to Mr Broadbent—asked to give message to Dad—said saw him and spoke to him before coming.

Church today—hope every Sunday. Fish load this evening. Mrs Howell:– 'Do you know someone was trying to get an intro? A nice young chap.'

'Really?' I said but I knew.

'I'm not joking. He was watching you most of the time and asked if I knew you.'

'I'm flattered,' I told her and passed it over lightly.

Mrs Dowland died about ½ past 7 p.m. Decided to send prize to Shakespeare—being very rash—hope he doesn't think I'm throwing myself at his head—just feel a kindly and curious interest in him—pity I don't know his wife.

Tuesday, 6 June 1944
Tuesday and Friday classes. Mary Marks 20 today. Rained about 6 a.m. and all morning with gentle drizzle evening. Spent morning at the Summers—cards and was teased. Dan came round—gone very thin—smartly attired—did not speak to

me. Joyce said getting her own back—teasing Joan Marks about him. Joanne and Dia quarrelled—later refused to service. Asked Miss Stewart to take me on when in need of helpers in hospital. Wrote and sent to Shakespeare.

Thursday, 8 June 1944

Borrowed gramophone—dancing on steps from 6–½ past 6 p.m. also from 9–10 midnight—enjoyed it—Joyce improved marvellously. Two 'Spins' [guards] came— 'Mickey Mouse' and another who was drunk—former brought his dog—was singing—drew maps and I gathered—fighting in India—Br many die—'Balsom' drunk too—was eating remains of fish loaf outside. 'Grumpy' and another spoke to me—quite sane—'Balsom' spoke pretty loudly in Joanne's shack. Yesterday men told to pull all Kajang down in front of us—delighted and better view. Today *all* round Camp taken down—wires in place—good view of Men's and our Camps—don't like it as reason not known. Rumours—meeting today or tomorrow—no changes in Camp until 3 months over then those asked will be released and others away—going to Woodlands. Saw Professor Hopkins walking about—wonder which is Hut 40—no letters today. Mrs Bryant's birthday today.

Saturday, 10 June 1944

Rumours—over 50s and 'non-bearing' allowed to live together!!! 'Toothbrush' gave some sweets to the children. Spoke to Dia who asked if could be allowed to keep some hens. Saw heavy smoke from the rubbish heap—very uneasy and unable to sleep. Then heard shouts—got up and saw fire had started in the rubbish heap. 'Balsom' came down from the hill yelling to throw water on it. Didn't take long to put the fire out—wonder how it started—hope not going to be an inquiry tomorrow.

Friday, 16 June 1944

Aunty Maud in hospital again. Mrs Gordon read bits of her letter from her sister-in-law—apparently outside world knows very little about us. Last night 'Balsom' came over and shook my bed—had a fright and wondered what he wanted—had something bright in his hand—for a moment thought it was a knife. Frightened, I drew myself into the bed—'Bodoh!' (stupid) was all he said and stretched out his hand. Realised he was offering me something—gingerly stretched my hand— 'Ah, ah, good, good' was all that was said and left, laughing to himself. It was a jar with pickled leaves of some sort—must have been his way of saying thank you for putting out that fire the other night. Tasted a bit of it and gave the rest away—it sure was 'pickled'.

Sunday, 17 June 1944
Meeting 3–4 p.m. Dad's got Pellagra—taking Marmite and not doing any work. Had good meal—lots of fried rice! Allowed to send cablegram—sent one to Aunty Grace. Blackout tonight and I believe I heard sirens in the distance.

Saturday, 1 July 1944
Came out of hospital yesterday. Malaria again with temperature between 103–104. Taking large doses of quinine—awful, feeling really sick—not eating. Not allowed to start work yet—to rest for 4 weeks—good gosh! Me rest for that time—impossible! I'd go mad—what am I supposed to do all that time? Write, of course, if I can get more paper.

Saturday, 15 July 1944
Started working in the garden today—while digging to plant sweet potatoes found a worm—fat, worm—picked up the wriggling thing and a thought came into my mind—wonder what it would taste like? Didn't fancy swallowing the squirming creature—threw it away—then found a clod of earth with more of the pink worms—had an idea—collected a tinful and later took it to the hut—decided to cook the worms and see what happens—well! All that was left after the cooking were thin strips of dried-up skins—not appetising—but hunger took over—took a bit of a piece—not that bad—a sprinkle of salt and it tasted like bacon rind— well, I imagine that's how bacon rind would taste—crackly and salty! Did I tell anyone?—No way! They might think I've gone 'cuckoo'—eating worms indeed— what next?

Thursday, 20 July 1944
Did a dreadful thing today—thoroughly disgusted with myself—I swallowed a baby mouse! Found a nest of baby mice in the lalang—so tiny and pink and helpless—I was so very hungry after working in the garden and food was getting scarce. Without thinking I scooped up one and popped it in my mouth and before I realised what I had done, I swallowed it. Immediately I stuck my finger in my throat to make me sick but it was gone and I did feel a bit green after that. Afraid I was very subdued little person and felt really awful about the incident—how could I have done such a thing and I couldn't even tell anyone about it. I don't even want to think about it and even the worms have lost their attraction—I feel sick!!!

Thursday, 27 July 1944

Hugh Fraser died yesterday—very sad. He and another man came back on the 24th—one was carried on a stretcher and the other was able to walk with assistance. Still no news of Mrs Nixon.

Had another bout of malaria—Aunty Maud threatens to chain me up and Dr Williams thinks she'd better hide the 'Chunkal'. Jeannie wants to murder me and put me out of the way—all because I refused to go to hospital!

Saw notice

Death of Mr Hugh Fraser—Mr Hugh Fraser was returned to Camp from Military Police Custody on 24th July, 1944. He was suffering from dysentery and was in a dying condition. Medical attention including a blood transfusion prolonged his life until 7.30 p.m. on 25th. When asking permission to nurse I pointed out to the Nip Officer in charge of the Camp that after the war we would be asked many difficult questions by our government if he died. The officer told me he had no authority to give such permission but would refer to the High Command and give me an answer the next morning. When Mr Fraser died I represented to the Nip Night Duty Officer that the Camp wished to observe a day of mourning and to do none but the essential camp fatigues on Wednesday. He tried twice on the telephone to obtain consent for this but failed. Early on Wednesday morning the Nip acceded to a request that outside fatigues start at 9.30 to allow workers to attend the funeral service. When the Acting Camp Supervisor and Mr Tominara arrived they told me that although they realised the high position Mr Fraser had held they were sorry no special treatment could be accorded because there are represented in this Camp many nationalities besides British. Only one lorry was available for the funeral but as many mourners as we like could go on that one. Other friends could parade at the gate and pay their respects as the coffin passed.

Mr Tominara was at the gate when we left and saluted respectfully as the lorry passed. Mr Kanazai uncovered and bowed at the graveside at Bidadari.

There were 21 wreaths altogether—one specially made by Mrs Dickinson as from his wife and family.

Saturday, 29 July 1944

Was asked to collect money to buy a clock from Hut 1—wrote 'A collection is being made in order to buy a clock for the use of Cameron's Kitchen. It is proposed that each individual contributes five cents towards it. Those willing will have their names drawn, the ownership of the clock which she is entitled to, take with her *when we leave this place* (broken or otherwise! That depends!)' Collected $1.35 cents.

Monday, 31 July 1944
Yesterday had urgent call from Matron Stewart—wanted me for VAD work so worked from 12–2 p.m. Mrs Daley showed me what to do—not working in the garden—back to being office-runner and to do VAD work every second day.

Allowed to send out postcards but with only 25 words. Sent one to Mr and Mrs C.D. Demetriades and to Fidelis.

Wednesday, 2 August 1944
Mrs Attias died last night. Had new buns this evening sandwiched with fish paste . . .

Friday, 4 August 1944
Mrs Wemps begged me to write a poem to send him [Mr Murphy] with a present . . .

Sunday, 6 August 1944
Not feeling too good today—head and body aching—surely not malaria again! Meeting changed to today 3 to 4 p.m.—hope feel a little better then . . .

Thursday, 10 August 1944
It's my birthday and I'm twenty today. Elaine Bryant made a birthday cake as a present—must have been saving some of her rations.

Bloom and de Mowbray invited us to 'elevenses'. Lizzie had a part too—together we had a 'fun' time—there were flowers and more flowers as presents—a real 'Say it with flowers' theme. Shared my birthday with all—it tasted good too—thank you, Elaine.

Our first baby boy was born yesterday in this Camp. Had birthday cards from across the way—Dad sent one as well.

Friday, 11 August 1944
The first baby girl born here today. Has been raining since yesterday. Dr Moricur died. Heard gula to be issued free. Permission given for meeting between friends other than relatives . . . Another request for more verses . . .

Tuesday, 15 August 1944
Recovering from malaria. Mary came to see me sometimes but today she is working and I won't be seeing her till tomorrow. Time on my hands again—having trouble getting paper and books to write on. Life in this Camp less restricted—can spend more time writing in my diary—but have to keep writing small to save space . . .

Sunday, 27 August 1944
What a life, what a life! Yesterday had fried rice—it was really good—enjoyed it very much. Today Joannie gave me an egg—what a forgotten luxury—shared half of it with Annie, my good friend. Saw Dad today—he seems to be getting weaker and weaker and sometimes finds it hard to talk.

Monday, 28 August 1944   **Stiffy White's birthday**
Made up a verse for her—'A Memory' to Mrs White on her birthday . . .
    Presented the poem with a little posy of flowers picked from the garden early this morning.

Tuesday, 5 September 1944
Dreadful day—6 girls and Mother Begg on their knees in front of the Flying Dutchman—apparently one of the girls was slapped and that the girls were seen stealing.
    Begg dismissed at lunchtime but the girls had to stay without lunch until 3 p.m. 'Blue-stocking' arrived unexpectedly—told Mrs Chowns to call the father of one of the girls. Thrashed the poor man and broke his stick. Then told him to get down on his knees and had him whacked dozen of times till he fell on the ground—still 'Blue-stocking' hit him—the daughter was in hysterics and she screamed each time the stick fell on the man—Mrs Chowns pleaded for him and at long last at her request told the man to go. Was assisted back to his Camp—body covered in weals. Eye witnesses including myself in tears—we felt so helpless—to strike a helpless man and especially when lying on the ground—it's so brutal, so inhuman—how could one human do that to another? Dear God, what have you let us in for? How could you let it happen—how much longer?
    This incident made us all wary and I must be very, very careful that I don't get caught writing this. In fact I don't know how much longer I can continue to write—am having trouble getting another exercise book and have to resort to writing as small as I can—no more ink so looks like I will have to be writing in pencil again.

Thursday, 14 September 1944

Mrs Shelton Palmer died 7 a.m. this morning—wreaths galore—funeral at 2.30 p.m.—own coffin. Two days ago Bill Aherne who was one of the entertainers of our Camp died—only 41—with dysentery, malaria and the rest!

Mrs Broadbent was operated on for appendix on 3rd September but is much better—will be out of hospital soon. Poor Elaine Blackman in hospital with septic sores. Having eye trouble again—am told it's eye strain! Had second inoculation. Saturday 9th we had the Children's Fancy Parade—the Men's band came over—it was a success.

Sunday, 24 September 1944

Been raining heavily past few days—no gardening—slept inside but still got wet. Have been looking after old Miss Jackson—very trying at times, poor old dear. Have been hearing about meetings under the road bridge—all hush, hush of course—they'll have to be careful not to get caught in the act—arranged for a whistler as a warning if Japs are about—all very well planned.

Sunday, 8 October 1944

Having a week's break from hospital duties. Meeting—saw Dad—looking much better again. Postcards permitted to outside world—sent one to Auntie Grace. This afternoon feeling sick and aching all over—had blood test taken and have landed in hospital. What a way to spend my week's break!

Monday, 23 October 1944

Came out of hospital this evening. Spent four days in ILA not the place for me and glad to be out. Glennie came over with the band to sing—not a bad voice but prefer John Hatyer's and Stanley Cottrill's voices. Getting letters from Gerry—most amusing.

Annie and I sharing the work in the garden—looking good too. We do have fun together . . .

Wednesday, 1 November 1944

Exciting night! Last night was Halloween's and what going on! Had a fright when woke up during the night—suddenly confronted with a 'Death's Head'—then a burst of noise of howls and screeches and dancing skeletons. Thought had a nightmare until Jo started to laugh with calls of 'Halloween, Halloween'!

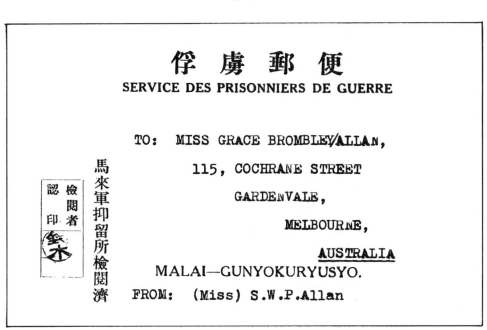

俘 虜 郵 便

SERVICE DES PRISONNIERS DE GUERRE

TO:　MISS GRACE BROMBLEY/ALLAN,

115, COCHRANE STREET

GARDENVALE,

MELBOURNE,

AUSTRALIA

MALAI—GUNYOKURYUSYO.

FROM:　(Miss) S.W.P.Allan

馬來軍抑留所檢閲濟

檢閲者

認印

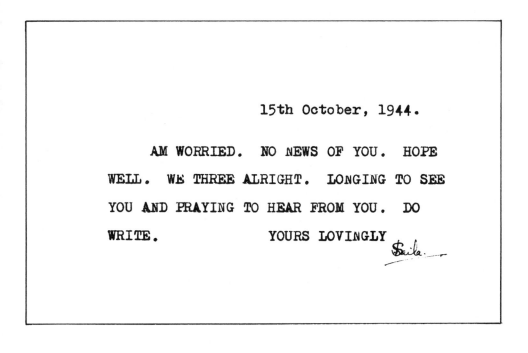

15th October, 1944.

AM WORRIED. NO NEWS OF YOU. HOPE
WELL. WE THREE ALRIGHT. LONGING TO SEE
YOU AND PRAYING TO HEAR FROM YOU. DO
WRITE.　　　YOURS LOVINGLY

Sheila.

Tuesday, 7 November 1944

Heard loud clapping—someone shouted—'Mrs Nixon's back'—walked to the Flying Dutchman, then carried on stretcher to the hospital looking very thin and white but cheerful, even managed to wave to us. What excitement as we lined in front of our huts as we welcomed her back. Another man also returned and permission given to sisters to nurse him from 8 a.m. to 8 p.m.

Thursday, 9 November 1944

Jeannie's birthday—gave a little embroidered square material. On Sunday there were sounds of AA and saw planes overhead—around 9.45 a.m. heard a siren—did we have a raid, I wonder. Later told that all garden fatigue to stop tomorrow. Mrs Nixon still on the SI [seriously ill] List. Fossy still in hospital.

Monday, 13 November 1944

'Fire, Fire!'—part of kajang caught fire this morning—burning of lalang too close to the fence. Hut 1 to the rescue—some from Hut 8 came over with buckets of water, etc. Not too much damage—notice to lalang gang to be more careful.

Mrs H's daughter returned from Mental Hospital and died 9.30 a.m. Mrs Howell in hospital with bronchitis.

Wednesday, 15 November 1944

Miss Jackson died yesterday at 4 p.m.—went across for the service this morning—very touching and the hymn 'Abide With Me' made me cry—at last she is at peace and in no more pain.

Friday, 17 November 1944

Mr L.H. Gorsuch back from MP custody and is in hospital. Mr John Gardner of Hut 15 taken to Singapore by order of General Saito for some office work—assurance given in presence of Men's Representative of well treatment and if not able to do the work to be brought back to Camp.

Sunday, 26 November 1944

Had the 'Glee Singers' to entertain us—conducted by J.L. Woods who also composed the last song which he dedicated to his wife.

Now able to send postcards out except to Japan and occupied territories! Seems to be a lot of air activity especially on the 20th.

Tuesday, 28 November 1944
'Balsom' drunk again. I had just gone to bed—Maureen did the disappearing act calling out 'Sheila, teadock!' (sleep). 'Balsom' lifted net and shoved something cold—papaya! A big, ripe luscious one! Went away and came back later with a packet to give to Jo! This morning cut the fruit up and quickly shared with the others—it was lovely! Afternoon—sirens—practice it seems though a lot of us thought otherwise.

Dr Williams and Mrs Eisinger

request the pleasure

of the company

of...Miss..Sheila..Allan...

(with her stool and mug)

between 1 p.m. and 2 p.m.

on

Saturday December 2nd, 1944

at

1. Sime Road.

Saturday, 2 December 1944
Maureen, Dr Wills, Elkins and Sowerby all had birthdays—had party in the hut about 32 of us—a good time was had by all of us.

Friday, 15 December 1944
Came out of hospital—in with malaria again. Mrs Lindsay died. Having many ARP—no meeting because someone not obeying rules regarding lights out. Xmas preparations getting underway. Allowed to have three people for Xmas including relatives. Dad has been in hospital but much better now.

Saturday, 23 December 1944

Orders—from 18th Roll Call morning and evening but so far had only two. Has been raining—gentle drizzle this past week. Have been spending time writing short stories and verses—keeps me occupied and diverts attention from my diary.

Monday, 25 December 1944

Xmas Day! Last night had Carol Service in the Orchard—it was absolutely beautiful. Meeting from 2–4 p.m. Mingled with the others in the Orchard. Had cards from a few of the boys—a nice one from Gerrie—he is so shy and what lovely eyelashes he's got! There's Mr Hogg—a quiet fellow. Glennie is a real flirt. Murphy—the sailor lad—shows his dimples every time he smiles. A very pleasant afternoon—a different Xmas to the ones we had in Changi. Here—it's fresh and green—open spaces instead of being confined by grey walls! Another Xmas, another year— wonder where we will be next year.

Notice from Men's Camp Representative

Lt Suzuki Camp Supervisor sent for me today and addressed me in the following terms:–

'You will remember that a year ago last October a considerable number of internees were taken by the MP for questioning in connection with certain investigations. As one result of these investigations Mr J.S. Long was tried by a M Court and found guilty of spying, for which offence he was executed on 27th November last. The Judge took a very serious view of this case, spying being considered a grave offence in all countries. In this instance of J.S. Long the case is especially serious owing to the fact that he took advantage of his privileged position during the course of his duties in bringing food and other necessities into Camp.

'General Saito has asked me to instruct you to warn the Camp of the seriousness of such actions.'

I felt it my duty to the Camp to once again warn all internees of the grave consequences which may attend the breaking of Nip instructions in appearing with any member of the local population.

Signed C.E. Collinge
Men's Representative December 15th 1944

Wednesday, 27 December 1944

Dancing party from 6–8 p.m. up at Fraser's in Kitchen—Mary played for us—also Mrs Attias and Ruby—Joan Hanson was too nervous. Jean White came and watched—saw that she would like to join in—so asked Hebe to take her round for the old waltz—after that took her round myself many times—was happy to see her enjoying herself. For the time being forgot I was in Camp.

The dance went with a swing when Miss Burgin came to play for us—asked for ½ hour extension—granted. The Auld Lang Syne brought the roof (?) down—it was deafening! Mr Brubel's jugglings defied gravitation when he balanced a glass tier on his forehead. The comedian (Mr Shadek) was most amusing. 'Susannah's a bonny wee sow' was hilarious! The tap dancing was something special. John Hayter again on the air for the children. The card and fan tricks kept us guessing—the drawings were, of course, cleverly done and the music was good. A lovely moonlight night—the Kluangs [fruit bats] have returned after months of absence and there was a right royal battle round the fruit trees the other night—they keep me awake the whole night with their shrieking.

1945

Monday, 1 January 1945

Meeting yesterday—rained but stopped in time. Celebrated new year with Dad—had a serious long talk—gave some papers in case of death—handed them over to Mum. Last night welcomed the New Year but not allowed to sing and make noise. Some of the girls planned to rob papayas and rambutans but one of the mothers gave the game away. At the stroke of 12 I led them to the Xmas tree—we circled round it, and joined hands and sang Auld Lang Syne under our breath.

This evening command came for a show—women to perform for the Nip officers and their honoured guests otherwise all privileges cut off—a four hour entertainment it is rumoured to be. We are asking fathers and brothers to come over if possible.

Thursday, 11 January 1945

'Air-citement' morning—'big and small birds and pop-guns too'. This show went on for several days. Dud shell found in Men's Camp. 15 more internees—7 of them Dutch. Mrs G. White died, also another man. A quarrel erupted between two females—a real ding-dong of a one!

Saturday, 27 January 1945

Plenty of 'air activity'. Yesterday ordered into trenches afternoon. Letter from Gerrie to say Dad is ill and so can't come to the meeting tomorrow and invitation to join him and family instead—what a nice, thoughtful gesture.

Tuesday, 30 January 1945

Maude in hospital again. A drunken brawl and Balsom's nose stitched by Dr Cameron. Internees to declare amount of money in their possession above $10. About 1,000 internees arriving from Singapore and upcountry because of bombing—possibly the harbour and Naval Base. Air raids daily—Cathay, Capitol and another building on fire a/c of Chinese Communists. Talk of repatriation again—lists of perm. invalids, children, over 65 and families to be compiled.

Thursday, 1 February 1945
'Excellent show' from above—batches of 4; 4; 10; 19; 6 and 3—lovely lot of 'eggs' dropped—came from somewhere SW and NE. 87 altogether from ½ past 10 to 20 to 12—last two batches a little N. The 19th had no 'eggs' and 3 opposite direction. Fire and smoke—seems like a 'good day's hunting'. A shrapnel found in Hut 12 garden (?)—missed hitting several people. Freddy doing another sketch of me. Rumours abound—(?) about 2,000 internees coming and huts being built for them with POWs helping—also internees from India and that we are to go to Hong Kong or Japan!

Saturday, 10 February 1945
Ration cut down—Children 7 ozs; Non-workers 8 ozs; Camp workers—10 ozs and Nip workers 18 ozs.
     Tomorrow special Roll Call—10 a.m. at Flying Dutchman in four groups—Br UK, Br Eurasian, Br Jews and Indetermines. Going to be a protest against Nip workers getting rations—after all they are not in Nip Internment Camp—we are!

Saturday, 24 February 1945
A large 'flock' (between 120–130) of silver plumaged birds dropped enormous 'eggs' at five places at least—dark mass of smoke rising in a huge column, higher and higher like a great moving snow-capped mountain—below orange sky—it was a grand sight—action at last! Seems like war has come back to Singapore—maybe the Nips (I hope) are getting what's due to them!
     Dad much better but still very weak on his legs. Am trying to sell a few of my things so I can buy extras for Dad. The Kluangs have gone again. Nips want money to bank for us—only $100 allowed on person.

Saturday, 10 March 1945
Died—Gilfillan—very sad—reports said much better—sorry for the girls—wrote letter of condolence . . .

Thursday, 22 March 1945
New interns coming on Sunday—no meeting and church but rumour that on Easter Sunday 2 hours meeting. Title—'Expectant Mother'—girl knocked senseless—affair with S/M Ton. Admitted to hospital in night—story of falling in bathroom—fainted—G. Raft found her—sister called him to her. Another—Olga in hospital shock of the night—story—taken to green cottage but drunk's words not accepted—

Mrs Kir returned—new huts getting on—one near us—very bad storm yesterday. Feeling lazy, and bored and hungry. Gula for sale—what a week! What a queue at Flying Dutchman! Late evening drizzled—many disappointed—two days later some more—at White House (Snow White's) again same thing—yesterday some more and went begging both at Snow White's and Flying Dutchman.

Maude's hands healed marvellously—wonderful! Concert on Saturday—very enjoyable. Liked the two pianists—Vincent Hay and Robert Eisinger—in fact the programme was very good though some were cut out. All must sew caps—a protest against Military work sent—Mum took on—food getting less and less—Cap workers get extras—Anna's chickens laying again—one night ate Spurs (jo's cock) was lovely but not enough. Nice evening. Feeling homesick and longing to talk to M—miss her so much—wonder what she now thinks of me—probably thinks I've got over it—but how wrong—I still love her and loving her more each day—only more silent in my love—what's the use, can't show my feelings and so very shy of her—she is so pretty and attractive—if only have the courage to talk to her—what wouldn't I give to hear her voice—to see her smile—Oh! I love her much too much! and it hurts!

Sunday, 25 March 1945

Rained yesterday and all day today—quarter to 9 baggage carriers and runners with the officials went to Green House—I followed later after VAD work—½ past 10—at first carried a few things but left off—stationed with White and Brooks—custom house—near gate.

Lorries and Police vans—Jews and Jewess mainly—others Indians, Malays, Chinese and a few foreigners—Christine returned—lot of flirting going on—was only a looker-on—helped to count and get names and show hut numbers. Once directed an old blind Jewess—some very pretty—a few taken to hospital on stretchers—saw some men I know. Gerrie tried to get a few words in but paid no attention—must be wild—very amusing though did not join the jostling—too serious for it—Jewesses names alike but no relations even to features.

C.P. Prichard did same job—Hegarty, White, Brooks, Maureen and myself stayed on full time—so Murphy brought up to us five buns for lunch—very busy day—also muddy and slippery one—many fell—one man did not want his two sons to have anything to do with the mother because 'she's a bitch' and to please look after them for him. One Malay claimed to have a husband by the name of Lang—must have brought the whole household—provisions galore—butter, chickens, fresh fish, rice, oil, ducks, dogs, gula, sugar, milk, tin foods and biscuits, chairs, tables, beds and beddings together with personal things—supposed to have 550 women and children but about 530 (nearest) only came—next bringing up country people—a mixed group all right . . .

Anna's father died—sad story—family (mother, sister and children) badly treated by Uncle and Aunt (a married one, not divorced—had lived for nearly 20 years). No Doctors coming in—wanted outside—felt quite superior to the other girls. No meeting today but rumour about 2 hours on Easter Sunday—no Church this morning. Now feel a little fagged out—Anna took me to see family. 'Brothel Houses'—Snow White's and Kitchen. From tomorrow to Sunday doing gardening—going to build more huts—men working very hard—Mary's brother—George, twin to Peter—came in—she's not feeling well—with temperature. Been having stew for tiffin for several days and hash with bun at night—very tired.

Wednesday, 28 March 1945
Monday, Tuesday no more [new internees] but today!!!—up-country—knew only one—married with babe in arms—not so well off this batch as Sunday's. Helped with names—with Maureen and Jean White and Brooks—better system this time—Red Cross parcels arrived—will be distributed soon—one per person for old internees and 1/5 for the new—bad days with rain—Hut beside us is No. 2.

Thursday, 29 March 1945
7 from Pahang yesterday evening and tonight about 100 expected—believed to be from Penang—9 p.m. nothing doing—train delayed and if arrive later will be put in Hut 29 till morning.

Friday, 30 March 1945
58 women and children this morning—a poor looking lot—a few with dysentery—one baby believed dying from it. Mrs Aitkenson had a stroke on 24th, Saturday and died on Wednesday 28th and Mrs Philips (newly interned) this morning—some very pathetic cases. Dr Smallwood in hospital and so is Isbel. Sacred music for both Camps this evening in Orchard. Confession tomorrow—High Mass for us in Orchard at about 10 a.m.—very nice—also 2 hours (2–4 p.m.) meeting on Easter Sunday.

Saturday, 31 March 1945
Rained evening so music postponed to this evening. Did not go—Sarah Manahan wants to see me—was in Amber Mansions—now have got a stable—not bad. A lot of fuss about moving from 5 people in Hut 5—refused to take punishment and Miss H was going to resign but it was not to be—punishment less severe

and vote taken for Miss H—'Confidence' or 'No'. In favour and staying on. Nice day today for a long time.

Last night saw a big fire but night before last (29th) about 3 a.m. had a surprise—woke up by bangs . . . 8 and sirens went—saw rosy flares and . . . so many of them—in the flares saw two silver 'birds'—real thrill—and sky was aglow—counted about 23 lots. It was good. No parcels given out because General could not be found. Am beginning over a new leaf tomorrow.

Sunday, 1 April 1945
Heard Fathers Ashness [three brothers] came in yesterday. Was glad and wrote to Father Rene asking about madam St Winifred. Had meeting—went to both services. Father Cosgrove gave sermon. Dad not too good—fainted yesterday—two Nips found him. Pellagra getting worse and he is having a lot of problems in remembering things and gets confused easily.

Wednesday, 4 April 1945
Had a busy day at hospital. Malaria and dysentery cases—Anna's mother in with the latter. Doctors, sisters and VADs have hard work now—not enough bedsheets, macs, bedpans, etc. Now 32 in our hut—as if we are not already overcrowded—tempers not improved by this situation and personal possessions are jealously guarded—naturally accusations are flung in all directions. What a bitchy lot of females we have become!!!

Thursday, 5 April 1945
3 biggest huts in Men's Camp taken over for POWs (Dutch—Indians???) Heard KL and Penang badly bombed. A lull from 'invading' new internees! Thank goodness for that—Hut 2 is now fully occupied. First time no rain yesterday after 59 days of wet weather! Parcels still not given out—supposed to be for Easter but General had gone away. Not feeling too well today—I think 'Lady' malaria is going to pay me another visit.

Sunday, 15 April 1945
Came out of hospital yesterday. Went in on Friday 6th. Thought malaria but it was dysentery—lost weight again and feeling weak in the legs. Dad went in hospital too but came out two days ago and is now in the Convalescent Unit. Anna handed me a note from Glennie asking me to see him—did not want to see him and

said so. However, at the meeting I saw Dad—he had a cut on his forehead, a black eye and a sore hand—asked what happened—could not remember.

This evening Anna asked what happened to Dad—told her he had fainted and hurt himself. She made a wry face—'I wonder if I should tell you . . .' Caught a note in her voice and knew something was wrong. 'Tell me what, Anna?' I asked. She was reluctant to continue . . . 'I think you'd better tell me, no matter how bad it may be,' I said gently.

'Jack told me what happened last Sunday and when Glennie wanted to see you I thought it might have been about your father' she stopped. 'Go on, please'— and then I learnt the truth of Dad's faint. 'He was given a bad hiding,' Anna whispered, fearful of the walls around us whose ears are always on the alert.

'A hiding? but whatever for and from whom?' I asked.

'From one of the men—apparently your father took a knife belonging to someone—the owner saw it and hit him pretty badly and he had to be taken to hospital.' I was shocked and bewildered at the thought that Dad had a knife with him—what ideas could be running in his mind! This is the second time Dad has been in a sort of disgrace—is he responsible for his actions? I've noticed lately that he rambles a lot about the past—not making much sense really. He seems such a child in his manner and I am worried about his mental state . . .

Letter to Mum from Mr P.B. Marriott

Dear Mrs Allan

It has struck me that you might be rather anxious about your husband due to his having been transferred to the Old Men's Hut. I have seen him—also Dr Hopkins who is in charge of the Hut and hastened to advise you that there is nothing seriously wrong with your husband.

Depressed he certainly is and it is this as much as anything which has brought on this present state of low mental action. He feels he can take no interest in anything and does not wish to be bothered much with people—a very natural outcome of our present life here!

I shall keep in touch with him and also Dr Hopkins and hope to let you know weekly how your husband gets on.

It was too early for Dr Hopkins to express any opinion but she fully expects your husband to benefit greatly by his admission to the Ward where Orderlies can help and he can be looked after and cared for so much better.

Dear Dad, to think the war has done this to you. Please God, take care of him— he doesn't deserve this—help him please.

Monday, 30 April 1945
Red Cross parcels given out last Monday 23rd. Had meeting from 10 a.m.–12 midday and then extended to 1 p.m. General about—photos taken—new internees allowed in. Band playing music and again in the afternoon. From 2–4 p.m. parcels given at the Cross Road. Dad did not turn up—am really worried about him—wish the War would end soon or malnutrition and disease will finish the lot of us! Food cut down again. Joke of the day—'You will now proceed behind Hut 1 and strip systematically from the bottom upwards and the men will follow behind with tools' referring to the land to be cleared of lalang! Almost as good as the one heard in Changi—'As the men will be here this afternoon will you ladies please take off all your clothes'—referring to the clothes line the men were going to take down for (?) repairs!

Monday, 14 May 1945
Rumours, rumours and more rumours of peace and going out. More parcels given out. Two men—Graham White and Loveridge died. Saw Dad yesterday—had small towel wrapped round him—looking ill—unshaven and uncombed—worried about him and afraid for him—told Maureen and Fossy and both advised to speak to M. Anna seems to have forgotten me—I am alone! News-y—on 7th May—peace-y with Germans, country divided into four sections—2 for Russia, 1 each for Merican and E-land. Army occupation for 10 years. Java and Suma in Br hands—heavy fight in Mau—'birds' to drop 'eggs' over Nippon if resist. Food still bad—'Slush and Ash' as some call it. Now away from window after so much fuss—more private.

Letter from Mr P.B. Marriott

Dear Miss Allan
          I saw your Dad again yesterday and found him very cheerful. He said he felt much better, as no doubt he will also have told you when he saw you last Sunday.
     Dr Hopkins has every hope that he may quickly recover as soon as a more normal diet can be obtained and we all hope that will not be very long now. He told me you are very interested in nursing and hope to make this your profession. If at any future time I can be of any assistance in helping you to attain this end please let me know.

Monday, 21 May 1945
Have been ill all the week—6th attack—nursed in the Hut—everyone very kind—did not go the meeting. Told M about Dad and said would see what can be done

and before she left she said 'You will go!' with a look that made my heart leap and I nodded. Am called, 'That slit-eyed Chink!'

Have been busy writing—wrote 'Cousin George', 'Bonnie' and 'The Marriage-Bed'—the last could almost be said to be rather crude but the story is there. Next one—'Comrades Three' and hope to finish 'Flame of the Forest'.

Tuesday, 29 May 1945

Went over to see Dad—nice place, view and breeze—met W. Williams—a nice old gentleman—said first lady spoken to for nearly three years. Dad not looking so good—weaker—afraid for him if not out quick.

Feeling much better but had a rise of temperature again—saw M who told me I was naughty to give her the cheroots and not to do it again—told her and said to come and see her in Dispensary—will give Vitamin tablets—which I'm going to give to Dad instead—funny even when M gives me aspirins—I keep them for someone else who may need it—like doing good but I suppose not fair to myself.

Pleased with 'Flame of the Forest'—putting into booklet and sending to Reverend Colin King to criticise and if all well—giving to M as birthday present.

Rumours always. Have been dancing late evenings—an enjoyable change. Did not after all send it to Colin King.

Saturday, 9 June 1945   Dad died today

I had just finished my shower when Maureen came with the words—'Get ready at once and go over to the Men's Camp. Your father has had a seizure.' I needed no explanation. I hurried over to Mum's hut—she was crying. Dr Winchester and 'Goran-pa' [a sentry] were waiting to take us over. Arrived in the ward—screens around the bed and I saw Father Cosgrove come out from behind the screens. He came forward and spoke to Mum—could not catch what he said but when Mum let out a scream and turned sobbing to me, I knew—Dad had gone—too late for us to say goodbye. Together we peeped round the screens but were quickly ushered out. Took Mum to a chair on the verandah—wanted to go and see Dad but she held on to me. Father Cosgrove came and spoke of Dad—of his wanting to be baptised and apparently had expressed the desire to become a Catholic several months ago. Father had instructed him and found him a willing pupil. Today he was sent for and when he arrived Dad had just passed away and he gave him the last blessings and baptised him. I thanked him and took Mum back to her hut.

Tried to remember Dad as he was but tears kept clouding my eyes. How I wished I was there before he died and even after death. I would have liked to have been able to touch his face and hold him close to me and to say that I love him and wish him goodbye. Oh, Dad—sorry we were too late to see you. Are you at peace and looking down at us poor mortals? I'm going to miss you, oh so much—and there is so much I wanted to say but most of all I want to say 'I love you, Dad. Goodbye—rest in peace, Dad'.

He is gone—no more will I see his face, hear his boyish laughter, see his many tricks of expression—his jokes, his loving arms around me. It is so hard to realise that I won't be meeting him again in the Orchard—bringing him extra food—he was always hungry and always enjoyed the food such as it was. But now—he will no longer be hungry, no longer be plagued with sickness. Dear God, thy Will be done.

So, Dad dearest, Mum and I say 'Sleep now and be at rest for always'.

The funeral service is set for 11 a.m. tomorrow.

Sunday, 10 June 1945

Today I awoke, heavy-eyed—everybody most kind. Went to Mass and Communion and prayed for Dad. After Mass was over, felt a tap on my shoulder and a voice whispered in my ear—'My deepest sympathy, Sheila. Come and see me when you feel like it and if talking will help'—it was Mrs Milne. Thanked Father Moran for conducting the service. There were flowers from all those who have gardens—Annie and I made wreaths yesterday and I asked Mrs Lucien Allen (our wreath-maker) to make a couple more—one from Mum and one from Auntie Grace.

The coffin was taken out to the cemetery—I don't know where. Too confused and too upset to ask—in fact, I can't remember much about what happened afterwards—all I know is that I haven't been able to say goodbye to Dad in the proper way—'Oh, God, how could you do this to me—what am I going to do without his helping hand. Please help me to understand and to humbly say Thy Will be done and to thank you for those precious years we've had together. Maybe, Lord, you know best.'

Mrs Cummings and Harrison took charge of Mum. I went over to Jean's and Mary's hut for comfort and quiet. Tears flowed at last! Finally I went to see Mum who was lying down. Her tear-stained face pulled me together—she needed comforting and so I held her close to me and together we let our tears flow freely—it helped to share out grief.

Later parcels were given out—how sad I felt as I opened them and almost choked at the sight of the food, thinking how Dad loved food, always talking about the parcels and so thankful at any extras given. It doesn't matter now as he won't be needing them again—ever again!

Womens Hospital,
11ᵗʰ June 1945.

My dear Sheila.

I heard late last night of your Fathers sudden death. I am so very sorry for you as a blow of this sort is worse when one is unprepared for it, and I am afraid you will feel very lonely for a time. Let me know if there is anything I can do, or, if you would care to come up and see me please do. It is quite quiet round this side even in visitors' hour.

With much sympathy,

Yours sincerely,

M. Elinor Hopkins.

Monday, 11 June 1945

So many letters keep coming over from next-door—keeping them for future reference . . .

Written a fortnight after his death—9th June, 1945.

Dad is Waiting for Me
(with apologies)

Dad is waiting for me over there,
In a land that is sunny, bright and fair.
He left me, oh, not so long ago—
Left me lonelier on this earth below.
But he's waiting, never fear,
Waiting until I appear

When my journey here is done
And I go out to follow on
Through the huge mantled door
That leads to rest and peace forever more.
He'll be there to laugh away
The loneliness I feel this day . . .
Why should I mourn if I'm left behind?
It'd be sadder if I leave here and find
Upon that other far-off shore
No one beloved who had gone before.
There'd be no one to welcome me there—
In that land ever bright and fair.
Just as when some long journey ends
I am awaited by smiling friends
Who watched for my on-coming train;
So shall Dad receive and welcome me again
Into that beautiful land so dear
Where we'll be together year after year.

Tuesday, 26 June 1945

Eclipse of the moon—not a total one—about 11.30 p.m.

'Mother's' birthday—gave flowers and the booklet (Flame of the Forest). Tunnels everywhere—rumours 4th July—starting the campaign—Prin. M. Rose is dead—Churchill resigned and Cripps taken on—Eden ill—hourly bulletins! Mum getting over it. Doing Sister Constance's work—2 hours morning and 2 hours evenings.

Wednesday, 4 July 1945

Nothing happened—workers get rice—Nip workers get rice and tapioca daily. Roll Call in age group for Friday 6th postponed—baggage and personal possessions confined—rumours of shifting. Doing Medical running this week. Mary's got a bad cold—lost her voice. Have not seen Marriott—ill in hospital.

Saturday, 28 July 1945

Doing gardening, reading and writing. No more Men's Lalang Fatigue—women now. Tunnels everywhere. 14th Camp punishment (only rice and water—i.e. buboh, watery stew buboh until further notice) because of thieving out in gardens. Anna unhappy—trouble with Lizzie. Maureen in hospital with malaria. Last Sunday did afternoon duty (12–4 p.m.) with Sully a/c of Mrs Murphy being sick—enjoyed

Bididari Christian Cemetery, Singapore, 18 February 1992. The flower marks the spot where my father was buried.

Elizabeth and Jack Ennis, taken at our reunion in Sydney after 50 years.

Mary Scarlett (née Trevor) and myself at our reunion in Melbourne in 1993, after 48 years.

it. Sully said will try to ask Matron to let me go on night duty—would love it. Another full moon is passed and 15 days more will be 21! Jackie Elias' concert—not too bad—last Saturday better. George de Broise invites me out—had been putting off for some time—rather like staying in—might as well go tomorrow and be done with it. Roll Call. Hut 23 punished—no meeting for two families a/c of laughing and giggling—thinks at him (Nip official)!

Sunday, 29 July 1945
Bangs and sirens! Been thinking of Dad and feeling sad and lonely again. Evening on steps with Jean and Mary—Miss Smith calls us 'Faith, Hope and Charity'! Now Nip workers get Camp workers' ration too.

Friday, 10 August 1945 – 21 today
Baby born to crippled Jewess—prophecy concerning her—a Jewess Rabbi dreamt that when a crippled woman gave birth to a boy we'll hear of Peace! Tunnels everywhere—just outside Hut one.

POWs working. Mum made curry and cake—have with Dav and Harri—gave some to various people. Saw M. Letter from Maureen in hospital . . .

Tomorrow having coffee with Mrs Corn. Rumours of peace—good news. Roll Call.

Saturday, 11 August 1945
Heard one of the POWs singing 'The war is over!'

Thursday, 16 August 1945

STOP PRESS

The latest—great excitement. POWs spoke to Hut 1—'War over on 15th'. Everything is over. Our military is taking over on 20th. 4 delegates and Stanley Jones are on their way to take over on 24th. All over the Camp—later not quite over. Felt ill—malaria and dysentery, also sore throat.

Saturday, 18 August 1945
Tunnellers in Camp told to pack up—also Nip workers—Nips told to pack up by 12 midnight except a few. Big feed—parcels (13 and 14 to one). Hospital nursing mothers and babies get ½ Klim [powdered milk]—great excitement indeed!

Sunday, 19 August 1945
CONFIRMED at last—all over. Deo Gratias! Cannot write more. Rain. Meeting.

Monday, 20 August 1945
Heard Church bells. PEACE! Saw our planes—a lovely sight and flying low. Feel both sad and happy. Roll Call—Yamato spoke—said in charge—to behave—keep what we think in our hearts—when he goes can do as we like! Chinese sending in eggs, butter, milk. Chinese living just outside killed two pigs and threw them into the Camp to us. Glennon very funny—quotes from books!

Tuesday, 21 August 1945
Heard that internees from Burma being sent home—the sick in three days and the rest in 27 days. Mary and Jean came to see me. Heard tomorrow Br taking over. POWs and internees got letters from husbands. Food, food and more food. Tootsie Turner went to new huts warning them that today Nips decided to fight to the last—why happy and joyful—war not over!

   Had rabbit pie. Wonder where Leslie is—if will see him again—feeling quite romantic about him! Heard at 12 midnight on Friday Union Jacks up all over Malaya.

Wednesday, 22 August 1945
Good tiffin—rice and real curry sauce—had also Rabbit—no more buboh now. Feeling better and longing for home on the mines close to Nature. Seemed Chinese brought in lorry of food but was turned away insisted but no go so went away but came back with Communists—our men tried to sooth things down but not until Nips threatened to shoot that they went away. Evening all Nips dressed in their best to receive the Br but they never turned up!

Thursday, 23 August 1945
Heard Sir Shenton Thomas in London—that Union Jack hoisted up at 7.30 a.m. tomorrow and that Orchard open to both Camps from 8 to 8.

Friday, 24 August 1945
Meeting 2.30 to 4.30 p.m. in Orchard—hospital tomorrow—meetings every afternoon. Both representatives with Davidson saw General Saito who spoke to them—Br troops coming to take over after 31st August. Sir Shenton Thomas last

heard in Mukden (?) war at end but negotiations still going on—try if possible not to create trouble by celebrations, singing of patriotic songs and wearing badges. At 5 a.m. Br planes over Singapore to drop parcels—Red Cross parcels given out today. Yesterday 'Acid Drops' praised Hut 5 and said will remember us in his heart—tears in his eyes—all Nips cried. Read circular about Emperor's speech—said he declared war on 14th December 1941 in their interest—millions have died by the new invention of bomb—the Atomic Bombs—needed two to end the war—one completely wiped out one island—lists to be handed in of relatives in POWs and where we would like to go—will be sent away—internees in Java and Sumatra will be released same time as us—news of importance will be given in Green House and supply of newspaper. Emperor also said to be united now—thousands killed—had said to fight to the last but that over now—obey the enemy that is defeat and surrender—no suicides, killing, raping, looting, Hari-Kari. Red Cross parcels between 5–2 towels, toothpaste, powder and toilet paper given—eggs and fish on their way—work up some internees to put sheets on ground—POWs—to receive parcels from the sky.

Saturday, 25 August 1945
Nothing happened—everyone very disgusted about things—heard took Hong Kong in 1¼ hours and took away internees during battle—also that Br plans coming any time after 5 a.m. not at 5 a.m. as stated—some think just purposely as mental torture or the General misunderstood the message—but then we are not the only Camp—there are about 60 others—we are about 4,900 and something—say 6,000 men, women and children.

Tuesday, 28 August 1945
Representatives with Davidson went out to town—inspection of Gen Hospital and Alexandra Hospital also the big hotels for internees to move in when Br taken over—radio to be installed in Camp—can tune to any station. Br will not arrive from 6–10 days. Individual parcels from outside. Heard dreadful atrocities in Thailand and Burma. Swetchia recognised IEC—supplies—Red Cross parcels intended for Borneo and Sumatra will be released to us—news bulletin issued to us of world events. A plane, supposed to be Chinese came low and dropped leaflets. Cards home and also cards to fill as to where we would like to go—had an argument with Mum—I want to see Auntie Grace and she doesn't. Anyway, she's given in but with a bad grace and humour. After all Dad did want me to go before war started—it was his wish and I'm going to respect that—God helping me—yesterday so worried, wrote a note to M asking her to spare me a few moments to help and advise me—said to go—also Maureen, Fossy and Sully—they ought

to know and I'm taking the 'bull by the horn'. Heard 9 Catalinas flying over tomorrow to drop food from Australia. See Shelton Thomas and General Heath in (?) Cheruy-King—fleet in Penang sweeping mines and arriving here on Sunday. Getting pineapples—1½ tins—remember when used to get 2 cubes in Changi and on Emperor's birthday 4!!!

Some more individual parcels came in.

Wednesday, 29 August 1945

Sweet potato and tapioca beds raked up. Swetchia coming to pay us a visit some time—POW meeting on Saturday from 2–4 p.m. in Orchard—wonder if Leslie will come. Also concert same evening—going to be the biggest show ever put on—hope to be out before then.

Friday, 31 August 1945

Great excitement—young uniformed RMC came in.

M said 'A visitor from Ceylon'—very young and shy and fairly mobbed by us—with several others from plane—paratroopers came to report on suitable airfield—horrified at the state of Men's Hospital and Changi Prison—12,000 in there—9,000 inside. A riot in Johore. Yesterday when *they* came great shouts heard—walked coolly into Green House—Nips agitated and in a dither—disarmed on the spot—also Sikhs. Radio in Camp—heard news last night. A thrill hearing 'Big Ben' chiming and in familiar words—'This is London calling'—what joy—gathered very little from news—as heard only end of it—something said about the leaders going to be tried by military tribunal for major war crimes—from USA heard about the POWs in Japan—was worse than Hell! Starved and brutally treated. Food and more food—today drawing in the Australian Red Cross parcels—were wool, knitting needles, powder puff, face cream, lipstick, toilet papers and sanitary towels, writing pads, dark glasses, etc. Had powder and puff. Today had iced drinks—was delicious—smokes came in—more individual parcels from outside. M afternoon came with a man taking down where we wanted to go. M said Australia for me and nationality Australian. 3 others joining Nursing.

Dr Williams spoke to Matron who said could start as soon as we get out in Gen Hospital. Now wondering whether best to train in Australia or stay here. Hoping to see Marriott tomorrow. Meetings every afternoon and evenings (6–8 p.m.) in Orchard. Music and dancing—want to come out of hospital but dare not ask M. Mum reconciled to idea of my going away—Dan had written to me. Feeling rather sad in midst of laughter because of thinking of M—soon, very soon we will part, perhaps, never more to meet. I must pluck courage to ask for her address and her photo—there is a pull at my heartstrings each time I think of that day. Oh, M you won't realise how I will feel when the time comes—M of my Dreams, I'll never forget you as long as I live—I shall always breathe a prayer for you and wherever you are, I shall always be at your side in spirit.

Sunday, 2 September 1945
Heard from radio that Sir Shenton Thomas and several others are in Calcutta—4,507 internees in all here—gate opened at our hut—men and women walking out to the village—great activity there. Chinese from nearby kampong selling eggs, coconuts, bananas, chicken, etc.—grand fun. Am told next to go when bed wanted—wish was allowed to go. Dan sent an egg—a beautiful, big, fresh duck egg through Xenia. Everybody excited—1,000 Australian paratroopers supposed to land today—also today the signing of peace in Tokyo Bay on board the battleship 'Missouri' at about 10.30 a.m. Given iced drinks, ox tongue, milk etc, plenty to eat now!

Monday, 3 September 1945
Hoisting of Union Jack today.

Tuesday, 4 September 1945
Heard 3 cruisers ('Nelson', 'Cleopatra' and 'Sussex') and four minesweepers—the rest of the fleet coming in tomorrow. POWs visited relatives and friends (business). A group of sisters and doctors had photos taken by an officer in front of Hut 8. Yesterday gave M some fruit. Today had a tiny cup of brandy syrup and some biscuits and gave them all to M—glad for her to have it—came and thanked me (if only she wouldn't). Fossy came in hospital. Hoping to go back to hut tomorrow. News—off Singapore yesterday Br minesweepers finished cutting a path through the minefields for the ships which will bring the Occupation forces. The cruiser 'Cleopatra' which is the 1st big Br warship to call at Singapore sailed off yesterday to meet the 'Sussex'. Landings on Kyushi Island began yesterday—no incidents occurred. General MacArthur commanded Jap Army to report at once location of all POW Camps and to turn them over to highest ranking prisoner in each location—this officer to be given full authority to demand whatever he required in food, medicine and supplies. Emperor Hirohito from the Golden Throne spoke to his people:— 'All names of Japs responsible for ill treatment of Allied Prisoners of War are being added to the "War Criminals" list—in Burma, somewhere North of Rangoon 10,000 Jap troops holding out—arrangements being made for Jap officers to visit the area instruct the troops and lay down their arms'.

Wednesday, 5 September 1945

M wanted to keep me in another day but begged to be sent back to the Hut so came out this evening. Marriott came to see me—said to rest assured about finance—will keep all they can—was very nice—very kind and fatherly. Reverend Eales shaved off beard—seems that he was not recognised with one on. Union Jack hoisted above Hut 8 with cheers from all present—heard story of the union Jack hoisted in the Orchard on Sunday—it was the flag flying over Changi tower—Nips brought it down, trod, kicked and spat on it—ran swords through it and flung it away. One of the men rescued it and at the risk of his life brought it into camp and hid it. Later was carefully patched by the men with a certain woman's red petticoat.

Thursday, 6 September 1945

Last night went to the Orchard with Anna to Tom's tumble-down shack. Met Fred—looking fit, could hardly recognise him. Then an AIF chap came over—Anna had told me he was anxious to meet me—wonder what she said about me! Had sandwiches, coffee and bananas—all provided by Tom. Later went down to dance.

The young soldier's name is Lionel F. Young—nicknamed 'Darby'—said he's puzzled about me as I seemed rather vague in all my answers. Little does he know that I'm shy and not much of a talker—he must think me an unsociable creature.

'Are you afraid of me? or are you frightened of soldiers in general?' he asked.

'No!' I said.

Said something to Tom who replied: 'Oh, Sheila's always been like that' as if he knew me all his life!

Anna: 'Yes, she's very quiet but she's a great thinker'.

I bowed in mock courtesy.

Saw Bill and quickly moved out of his sight. Darby noted the evasion and wanted to know why. 'I try to avoid people I'm not too keen on.'

Silence! Then looking at me with a twinkle in his eye—'Do you like me?'

Could not help grinning back at him: 'Well, am I avoiding you?'

Had a final talk with Dr Williams: 'I'm wondering whether it would be better for me to train in Australia or stay here and train in the Gen Hospital.'

Dr Williams: 'Well, where do you want to work in the end?—in Malaya?'

I: 'I hope to work in Siam. You see, I want to do Health work, after years of experience, of course, there, and I thought that perhaps, it would impress the people better if I have a training abroad.'

Dr Williams: 'Oh, certainly! But I would advise you to get your general training here and then take a course in health work either in England or Australia. I know there is a college for such things and where girls from every part of the world go. So if I were you, I would do this. You'll find it a better plan as you will more or less know what line to take then.'

I: 'That's all I wanted to know and I'll take your advice. Doctor, thank you for setting my mind at ease.'

Doctor: 'It is just as well. Goodnight.'

I: 'Goodnight.'

Friday, 7 September 1945

Allowed to go into town but must be back by curfew (8 p.m.–8 a.m.). Went in a group. Town rather in shambles—buildings in ruins—smoke haze still around—being afternoon the whole town seems deserted!

This morning May and I went walking round the Camp—went to the kampongs nearby—up the hills and came back by the main road. Came back from town in time to hear the band from HMS 'Sussex' playing. How handsome and smart they looked in their uniforms as they marched up and down the Men's Camp, playing military pieces for 20 minutes. Then to the Orchard to play dance music. Lovely, especially 'God Save the King' we sang as we've never sung before. The roll of the drums, the voices—surely that melody must have reached and penetrated the very heavens to God. Tears came into my eyes—felt all choked up. Suddenly felt being pulled by the arms—to join hands with a small group—as we sang 'Auld Lang Syne'—others were crying too. Crying because we are free—crying because soon we'll be saying goodbye to the friends we've made in this 'Hell-hole'—tears and more tears—we hugged each other and we gave in to joyous laughter. How does one describe this feeling—something wonderful—touching, sad and yet joyous—oh, it's hard to describe this emotion that we all feel!

It is now half-past eleven—this evening was indescribable! Darby did not turn up. There was Buck, ex POW; Jimmy; Kyra and husband. Everybody was drinking except me. Jimmy danced with me most of the time—a good dancer and I enjoyed dancing with him. Then suddenly he said: 'Come, Sheila, let's get out of this crowd'.

Without waiting for my answer, he pulled me along with him—we disappeared in the darkness. Music grew fainter. Under some trees we stopped. 'Come and sit here for a moment.' There we sat in the dark—neither of us saying a word— Jimmy appeared deep in thought and so was I—it was good to be away from the noise and people milling around—sighed and a voice whispered in my ear: 'What's that sigh for?'

'I don't know—except it's pleasant sitting here . . .'

'With me?'

'Not necessarily' I answered back.

'Sheila, tell me about yourself.'

'There's nothing to tell.'

'Nonsense! I want to know all about you and what you are going to do when you leave here.'—spoke in a low voice that was slow with that distinctive Scottish accent. How I love to hear him speak—am a sucker for the Scottish brogue and glad too that he didn't know that.

'You realise, Sheila, it's over 3 years since I've sat and talked to a woman like this—it's a grand feeling, I can tell you. And I'm glad it's you I'm with.'

Felt uncomfortable somehow but tried not to show it—'Keep talking, Jimmy, please'.

Silence again—then taking my hands in his and I thought—those poor hands—how rough they've become!

'Sheila, what would you do if I kissed you?'

'No!' I said and quickly got up. Caught my left hand and laid his hot cheek against it.

'Why not?'

'What for?'

'What for?'—at that he released my hand. 'What for? You ask me that. God! You might as well ask why we live, why we are born? I'm sorry—you are so young—so innocent. Come, let's go back.'

Walked slowly back—stopped. Lifted my face gently—closed my eyes, thinking—Oh, God this is it—he's going to kiss me. Instead, he hugged me and I'm sure I heard a sob come from him—yes! I felt a tear on my cheek—looked up at him—he said nothing. Touched his cheek—there were tears! Put my arms around him and hugged him tight—don't know how long we stayed there—together—crying, crying! Somehow I didn't feel shy or awkward any more—walked me to my hut. Bent down and gently kissed my lips saying, 'Thank you, Sheila'.

'Goodnight, Jimmy.'

'Goodnight and I'll see you around, Sheila.'

As I watched him leave, I have this feeling that I won't be seeing him again—it seems as if he's saying goodbye.

Monday, 10 September 1945

Wrote to Miss Stewart, the matron. Reply:

'Miss Sheila Allan has worked as a VAD with me in the internment Camp, Singapore. She worked well, and I think she ought to train as a nurse. I recommend her to be put on the list for an early vacancy.'

Letter from Mr P.B. Marriott

Dear Miss Allan

        It now seems that I shall be repatriated before I can contact Mr Mead. I have therefore been unable to arrange for finance yet since the banks are closed and likely to remain so for some time. However, I have spoken to several people including Dr Smallwood of your Camp who is seeing Matron Stewart if possible before she leaves. If she does not contact Matron, she will give you a letter of reference and recommendation. All are agreed that by far the best course for you to pursue is to become a probationer at the General and go in for Health work, as Matron said. At the moment the military are in occupation at the General and Dr McGregor (Senior Health MO) says applications for work, nursing etc. are more than there are at present vacancies for. He further says this state of things may continue for some little time and it is the wisest plan for you immediately to fix up to board at the Convent while things settle down.

I am therefore seeing Father Cosgrove this afternoon and getting him to help you in any way he can. I will furnish you (enclosed) with a letter personally guaranteeing repayment of expenses incurred in connection with your board until such time as the Hospital can take you on and Father Cosgrove will support my guarantee I think. This financial aid will also cover any expenses you may need until you are drawing a salary at the Hospital.

I do hope these arrangements fit in with your wishes—please write and let me know as soon as possible if there is anything else I can do—I do not expect to be leaving for a day or two.

I hate leaving like this without seeing you actually in residence and cared for as I would wish but orders are orders and apparently I must go as soon as possible.

Wishing you all the best of luck and assuring you of my help at any time in future.

Well, this is it—looks like my future has been mapped out for me. How do I feel about all this—I don't really know. Everything is still up in the air. At the moment I am just taking one day at a time—so much is happening in Camp and I don't think anyone really knows what he or she is going to do—except maybe to get out of here as soon as it is possible!

Tuesday, 11 September 1945

Darby hasn't been to see us—Tom said he didn't like 'to butt in'—fancy that! So Anna and I wrote to him and this evening got a reply . . .

Yesterday went to the reservoir and wandered about. (?) Lady Louie [Mountbatten] arrived while we were there. Came back in time to see the ENSA Show—terrific show!

Night before last, Tom, Maureen and I went to listen to the radio in the Men's Camp—Anna had gone out. It was near the power station on the way to the hospital. There was a bright light and many people sat along the hillside listening. Stayed for half an hour. Saw a beautiful sight on leaving—part of the hill was still covered in tapioca bushes. A gentle breeze was blowing—the leaves glistening in the light looked like a sheet of water with ripples dancing in the moonlight.

Today again went to the reservoir (9.30 a.m.) for a swim with the others. Later took a gramophone and records to the house where we danced—had tiffin and tea there. Jimmy insisted on dancing with me all the time—he's a real flirt but boy, can he dance—and that Scottish drawl, how I love hearing it!

Wednesday, 12 September 1945

This morning, most of the Camp turned out to witness the Victory Parade—it was the formal surrender by the Japanese officers to Lord Mountbatten on the steps of the Municipal Offices. The padang was packed with (looked like the whole population of Singapore was there) people. Planes, flying boats, transport planes, fighter planes and bombers (you name it, anything that flies) flew low and zoomed here, there. The army, navy were assembled on the Padang together with the band—the marines did look smart in their 'whites'. What a lovely sight—we cheered and we clapped and we hugged each other and cried and laughed and then cried again! The atmosphere was unreal. Those who were specially invited were in the Municipal Buildings. I was on one of the balconies with the others. The POWs were there too. Lord Louie arrived in great style—how we cheered and waved our hands. The band played and he walked round, inspecting and talking to the army and navy—one sailor fainted and had to be taken away on a stretcher. Seven Nip Officials then arrived—the Chinese roared their anger and wanted to rush at them but were kept at bay by the MPs. After the ceremony was over—they came out again and were taken away. The Flag (our beloved flag) was hoisted while the band gloriously and thrillingly played 'God save the King' followed by French, Dutch, Chinese and American anthems. Heard speeches— had photos taken. We cheered and danced and cheered ourselves hoarse. There was dancing in the streets—we were mad, gloriously madly happy—Time stood still as we let our hair down—for a moment we forgot those 3½ years as we went into a frenzy of dancing, singing—we are FREE, FREE, FREE! AT LAST!

Finally exhaustion took over—physically and emotionally! How we got back to Camp I don't know—I think we got a lift back—was too tired to think! and collapsed on my bed and knew no more! This evening had pictures showing in the Orchard but we (the Gang) decided to go to the Dutch Club in town—we had been invited by the RAF boys. Unfortunately I missed out due to having woken up too late to be ready in time when the boys came to pick the girls up in the gharry. So went to see the pictures instead—enjoyable but a bit long— maybe still suffering from the excitement of this morning! I was standing up when someone offered me a seat—we got talking—Arthur is his name and he had nursed Dad. After the show we walked back towards the huts—it was a pleasant night as we ambled along. Talked of many things. He is also a Scots—I sure can pick them . . .

I took the opportunity to see [Mr Marriott] so I could thank him personally for what he has done to help us and to wish him a safe passage home. He seemed upset at not being able to finalise everything himself but I assured him that I would be all right though a little apprehensive about being left on my own but I will survive after coming through all this! Thank you for caring, Mr Marriott . . .

Mum said she doesn't need my help any more as everything is all fixed up. She hopes to be able to go back to Ipoh in a couple of weeks' time—wished that I was coming too but realised that I had my own life to work out and so wished me every luck in whatever I intend to do. I think she's relieved in a way that she doesn't have to be responsible for me. I said goodbye as I'm hoping to get to Town tomorrow and see if I can get an appointment at the General Hospital—I'd like to be able to start work as soon as possible and so support myself and not be a burden to anyone longer than I can help. I do have doubts about my abilities— I'm not sure how the world is going to treat me—wish Dad was still with me to help and advise me. Dear God, help me to cope in a strange world—help me to learn all there is to learn and to be sensible in all things. This is going to be a 'learning' experience and I'm scared, really scared.

Sunday, 16 September 1945
Didn't go into town—being Sunday so will leave for tomorrow. But last night— last night, oh what a night and Dear Diary I must write it down while fresh in my mind.

Last night was invited out to join the girls at the Dutch Club. Jo was insistent about me going out . . . Well, I thought 'just this once' is not going to disrupt anything. 'Oh, all right but how am I going to get back if I'm not enjoying myself?'

'You will, I tell you, you will enjoy yourself—you like dancing, don't you?' I nodded—'So, there—there'll be lots of dancing and you won't run out of partners'. With that she ran off, singing to herself.

Now, Dear Diary, comes the extraordinary part of the evening—got off early to the Club—the boys took us in their gharry.

'This is Sheila' as I got introduced to Peter, a sergeant. 'Whoa! Why haven't we met before!' he bellowed out, his bright blue eyes twinkled.

'Hey! Pete! let us have a look in' came a chorus of voices from the others and one by one they edged in to be introduced. Everyone seemed to be in high spirits and in no time the dance floor was taken over by hundreds of dancing feet!

I found myself seated next to a young RAF chap who was content to watch the dancers doing their thing on the dance floor. Took a glance at him—dark haired, well built young man—noticed the square jaw and wondered what colour eyes he's got. Pete came to claim his dance—he danced well and the music was good—I thought to myself 'I'm glad I came'.

Once again I went and sat next to this silent young man. I got curious and I wanted him to take notice of me—imagine that! Me who is so shy of the opposite sex, wants a stranger to talk to me! With a drink in his hand, he was in deep conversation with his mates and completely ignored my presence. Then the others left to dance and we were alone at the table.

'Now, he'll be sure to say something,' I thought but I might as well be invisible—my move I guess—'Have you been here before?'

'Hmmm? Oh, here? No'—a man of very few words evidently—am I intrigued!

'What about Singapore? Like the place?'

'Okay. Better than India'—still he didn't look at me and I so much wanted to see his eyes!

'Been in the Service long?' I persisted—'I'll get you to talk even if I don't have another dance' I promised myself.

'Five years!' He sounded bored and gazed moodily at his empty glass.

'You dance at all?' I asked.

'No—why don't you dance with the other chaps?' sounded rude to me as if he meant to say 'Why don't you leave me alone?' must have a 'chip' on his shoulder.

I laughed—at last I'm getting some sort of a response so I persisted—'I like talking to you'—he frowned—his gaze still on his glass. 'But, of course, if you'd rather—'

'No!' he turned to look at me—a dimple appeared on his cheek, his eyes I noted seemed to be smiling and the colour—grey and as I looked into his eyes I felt as if I was 'drowning' in their depths—a strange feeling, an unknown feeling came over me—suddenly I felt shy—unsure of myself—I looked towards the dancers on the floor.

'Sure you don't want to dance? Your sergeant is giving me a nasty look.'

'He's not my sergeant,' I almost snapped back—I felt uncomfortable as if caught in the act of showing my feelings—feelings of what? I'm not sure.

'He's not? Well, then let's take a walk—I need to stretch my legs. Coming?'

Just like that! and I got up and followed him like a young puppy after his master. In silence we went down the drive.

'Why did you want to talk to me?' he asked. What a strange question. 'I thought I had made it plain . . .'

'Oh, sure you made it plain enough, I assure you,' I interrupted him, 'That's why.'

'But why?'

'Gee, do you want to know the reason for everything?' I asked. 'I was just amusing myself . . .' he stopped walking and spoke slowly as if I had slapped his face with what I had said.

'You don't mean that.' Somehow for some reason I had hurt him with those words.

'I'm sorry . . . you are right . . . I didn't mean that, I really wanted to get to know you . . . don't now ask me why because I can't answer that.'

I felt embarrassed and wanted to get away from him . . . his presence was making me uncomfortable. He must have sensed my intention as he caught my hand to stop me from moving away.

'I didn't catch your name' he said.

'Sheila,' I told him. 'What's yours?'

'They call me Jinx.'

'Jinx? Are you a jinx?' I asked.

He laughed and he looked real boyish then. Went back to the Club and got us a drink—I made a face as I tasted mine.

'You don't drink?' I shook my head.

'Okay, I'll get you some lemonade . . . will do?'

I nodded—grateful for his understanding and I was thirsty.

Arrived late at the Camp after the dance. Was standing up in the gharry as I like getting the breeze against my face, when the gharry took a sharp turn and I was flung off balance. An arm was round my waist to steady me—Jinx was holding me against him—at first I wanted to take his hands off but somehow it felt very comforting to be engulfed by them.

We were escorted to our huts—the moon had gone down and it was quite dark walking along the path. Caught my foot and stumbled a couple of times when I found myself being swept up in Jinx's arms—I was going to protest but again came that feeling that it was nice being close to him. He put me down when we got to my hut—casually and without a word.

'Thank you, Jinx and goodnight.'

He smiled, 'Goodnight. I'll be seeing you, Sheila.' He said, turned and vanished into the darkness.

And so I come to the end of my story. And do you know what, Dear Diary—I would like to see him again—wonder if I will. I think he's 'jinxed' me into feeling something I've never felt before and I'm not sure what that is.

Monday, 17 September 1945

Woke early this morning—to Jo's surprise.

'Hell! What are you doing so early—and where are you going all dressed up?'

Questions, questions!

'By the way, you sure made a hit with Jinx last night'—at the mention of this name I felt myself blushing and made a big thing at tying my shoelaces so Jo couldn't see my red face.

'I thought you want to know where I'm going.'

'All right! Where are you going?' I told her I was going to get a job at the General Hospital.

'But that's occupied by the military.'

'I know, I know,' I said patiently as to a child. 'I was told yesterday that the General is needing more nurses. So, I might as well go and apply for a job.'

'Good luck.'

'I sure need it' and off I went on a borrowed bike.

Sun was shining as I rode past my hut, huts 11 and 10 and on to the road—all the way downhill—faster, faster—felt free, free as a bird—almost wished I could fly away, away up in the sky.

Along Selegi Road, past the Cathay Building and up Stamford Road and into Hill Street. Before the bridge was the big Hill Street Police Station—still wearing its camouflage of dirty yellow, brown and green—remembering, felt a shiver come over me. The bridge—now New Bridge was lined by hawkers doing brisk trade even at this hour of the morning. Eventually came to the gate of 37th General Hospital. A guard inquired my business—told him and was directed to the main building. Had my letters of recommendation—handed them to the officer in charge. Got to see the Matron—must have been all right as I got the job.

'An ex-internee!—a bit soon to be starting work,' she said. 'However, we do need extra help so you'll have to do—can you start tomorrow? Say about 9 a.m. as you'll be travelling from the Camp—can't put you up at the moment, but will try and see what we can do later for you.'

Must have looked real happy at the prospect of working there—'You must be keen to start, am I right, Lass?'

I nodded.

'Be off with you and I'll see you right here at 9 a.m. sharp!'

I was dismissed. Pleased with myself and rode quickly back to Camp—the world seemed bright today and I feel glad to be alive—so happy that I found myself whistling—felt as if I could be kind to the whole world and I wanted to let everybody know that I'm just so happy to be alive!

Jo was waiting for me to come back and went in to tell her the news—she was glad for me but thought starting work tomorrow was a bit sudden.

'By the way, coming to the Dutch Club tonight?'

Was going to say no then thought why not make this a celebration but I know it wasn't only that—I wanted to see Jinx again—that is, if he'll be there and hoping that he'll be there too.

Tuesday, 18 September 1945

Am I tired tonight! Started at the hospital this morning—lots of sick soldiers—did plenty of 'blanket' baths for the patients; some had to be fed. Taking temperatures and giving medicines but no writing of reports, thank goodness! Lost count of how many beds I had to make by the time I was ready to be off duty. It was a forty bed ward and not a bed was vacant.

Made friends with 'Lofty' the little Irish wardsman and 'Shorty' as you can guess is a six footer Scots. Then there's 'Curly Top'—an Englishman with a mop of blond curls. Everyone was helpful and there was a lot of teasing going on between the three orderlies.

'Going Home?' Shorty followed me to the gate. 'You were in Changi Prison, I'm told. Rough, was it? How did the Japs treat you?' He was eager to talk.

'Considering all the stories I've heard about the other camps, I think it must have been the best one to be in' I said.

'Didn't they ill treat you?'

'Oh, yes—in some ways they were pretty brutal and it was scary—some of the men and women had a bad time when they were taken outside by the Secret Police.'

Stopped at the Guard Hut—a friendly voice greeted me—'Off home now, Nurse?'

A lovely smile lit his rugged face—returned his smile and Shorty let out a snort. 'What has he got to get a smile from you?' and turned to the guard, 'I couldn't get her to smile like that.'

'An ugly face, Lad, an ugly face' was the answer and I had to laugh then!

Jo was eager to know how my first day at the hospital went—

'Very busy and am I tired.'

'Too tired to go out tonight?' she asked. 'We are having a party for one of the boys—a birthday bash for him.'

'Yes, I'll come but don't know if my feet will let me do any dancing—they are a bit on the sore side.'

'Good.' Jo said—'I'll let you put your feet up—give them a good rest and a rub and you'll be right,' and off she went singing away—what a happy child!

Thoughts turned to Jinx—he didn't turn up last night at the Club and was miserable—all the time. I kept looking for him—even the music and the dancing didn't help me forget him. Will he be there tonight? I won't know unless I'm there, will I? So I'm going to be there!

Wednesday, 19 September 1945

Jinx did not turn up last night. Asked the sergeant about him—casually, hoping that no one noticed my interest.

'Where's Jinx? Isn't he one of your crowd?'

'Jinx has never been much for girls'—he laughed.

'What's funny?' I asked.

'Do you know we had to drag him almost by the ear the other night—he came on condition that we wouldn't introduce him to any girls. I saw you trying to talk to him and was surprised to see you two later walking together. Shall I tell him you asked after him?'

How do I answer to that without giving myself away?

'If you want to—I just wondered what happened to him—thought he might have been shipped home' and I don't even know where his home is—England, of course, but exactly where?

Another busy day at the hospital nursing some very sick Dutch POWs—what terrible brutes those Japs are! Those emanciated bodies!—I could count every rib as I sponged them and the ugly ulcers—how could they have been so treated when they are POWs? Worst of all I heard stories of our own POWs—something about being sent to Siam to work on the railways—later found out that thousands of them were sent to the jungles of Siam to build a railway for the Japs—that thousands died while doing it—some from cholera, dysentery, malaria and starvation and stories even of some of them being beheaded! Why, why so cruel, why torture them to such an extent—how they must have suffered and who could blame them if they hated the Japs. Only heard the soldiers talking among themselves—would have liked to ask for more details but they didn't want to talk too much about their experiences to outsiders like me. Sometimes on my rounds I hear them crying with the pain of their dreadful memories—wish I knew how to comfort them. The war is over, sure, but to these POWs—the war within themselves is far from over—I know a little of how they feel though I haven't gone through what they went through. How I wish I could help them in some way—perhaps I have—a little—in nursing them and being there when they want anything.

Sunday, 30 September 1945

Day off today—have had a really hectic week—thought I'd never make it through a week. A couple of the patients died and three shipped home. Curly Top has been a real help. Got on well with Sister and George and the other girls working there. Tonight going to the Club with Jo and the Gang—Jo seems to have a special RAF boy—I think she likes him a lot.

Haven't heard anything about Jinx—Jo tells me he hasn't been to the Club since that night we met. So—I guess he is no longer with the boys—gone home probably.

Monday, 1 October 1945

Have left Camp and stationed at the General Hospital in the Nurses' quarters. Makes it a lot easier—perhaps won't feel so tired now as don't have to bike to work and back to Camp every day.

Last night when we arrived at the Club saw Jinx sitting with two other chaps. Went over to say hello—he seemed surprised—

'Excuse me, boys. I'll be back presently,' and with that he propelled me outside. Stopped just outside the Club.

'Pete told me you have been asking after me—he reckons that you'd like to see me again—is that true?'

What could I say except 'Yes' and I felt my pulse racing and believe it or not I blushed!

'Why? I thought Pete was pulling my leg. Why do you want to see me?' he persisted with the question.

How can I answer that when I don't really know the reason for wanting to see him except that I just wanted to see him again?

'I don't know why I want to see you—I just wanted to see you again—that's all . . .' I finished the sentence rather lamely.

God, how did I get myself in such a muddle?

'I wanted to see you again,' he began . . . 'Never mind that—what I want to know now is when am I going to see you again.'

'Going to be rather difficult, Jinx, as I'm now staying in the Nurses' quarters at the General.'

'That shouldn't present a problem. I shall see you there instead.'

I thought—'he does want to see me again' and now a question nags my mind 'but why?'

'What about tomorrow?' . . . my thoughts were interrupted by his voice in my ear.

'I'm working shift tomorrow and not off duty till 8 p.m.'

'I'll be there around 8 p.m.—waiting for you. We better get back inside and you can have a dance—one dance, mind you—with your sergeant.'

'Wish you wouldn't keep calling him "my sergeant".' I was a little annoyed at his teasing. I preferred to be with him—what is the matter with me—why do I want to be with him—tried to analyse my feelings—hopeless! Could I talk to somebody about it? Who? Am not much good at talking about my feelings but I need to find out why I feel this, this way about Jinx and I don't even know how to describe this strange feeling! Dear Diary—I am all mixed up! Writing down doesn't even help.

Wednesday, 3 October 1945

Jinx arrived last night—was waiting for me as I came off the ward—told him to wait while I got changed out of my uniform.

Went for a walk, hand in hand—it seemed so natural somehow just walking, each deep in our own thoughts.

Yesterday spoke to Jo about Jinx and you know what she said?

'By the way you are talking about the boy, I think you've fallen in love with him.'

I was struck dumb for a moment—I couldn't deny it because I don't know what 'falling in love' is like—if she says that, then perhaps it's true. Can it be what I am feeling about Jinx is love? I've never been in love if that's how it feels because I've never felt like this before.

Dear Diary, help me while I think this over.

Thursday, 4 October 1945

Had an incident in the ward—one of the Dutch patients, recovering from dysentery made me really angry. While making his bed I caught a faint aroma of cooked prawns and onions—recognised the smell—'Mee Goring'—found the offending dish wrapped in a bundle of banana leaves. Did I go to town on the poor chap! I was so angry—all he said was that he was so hungry—just as suddenly I stopped being angry—I remembered I was hungry too—in fact I was always hungry when in Camp and hunger does strange things to people and I looked at him through tear-stained eyes—I felt his hunger but I also had a responsibility so I gently told him not to do it again and if he wanted more to eat to let us know.

Saturday, 6 October 1945

Last night stayed back on duty to care for another Dutch patient suffering from cardiac beri-beri—could see that he wasn't going to make it through the night. It was hard watching him gasping for air and trying to speak—wanted to make sure we'd let his wife know. There was little I could do except hold his hand and mop his brow.

'Someone wants to speak to you—a fellow called "Jinx" I think he said' Shorty whispered in my ear. Oh, gosh, I had forgotten him—he's been coming to see me each evening.

'Tell him, Shorty, I can't see him tonight and that I'll see him tomorrow.'

Three hours later the poor man passed away. Shorty and I busied ourselves with the last offices for the dead. I must have stumbled as I felt as if I was going to faint. Shorty was there to prop me up and slowly walked me through the ward.

Everything seemed still and silent, then I heard sobbing from behind a screen. It was Jimmy, an English POW.

'What's wrong, Jimmy—have you got a pain?'

'I don't want to die, please, I don't want to die.'

'Of course, you are not going to die. You are getting stronger each day and before long you'll be on your way home to your family. Think of that and say you are going to get better—you are going home. There!'

I cradled his head, burning with fever, until he stopped crying.

'But he died, Nurse, and he had what I've got.'

'Ah, yes, Jimmy but then he was a lot older than you and he had a lot more things wrong with him. You've got youth on your side, so be a good boy and start living.'

He smiled through his tears—'If you say so'.

'I do say so.'

Slowly I walked towards the Nurses' quarters—it had been a long day and night. I wanted to cry—no, I wanted Jinx but I had sent him away. Then I heard the whistle—a familiar tune 'I'll be seeing you'—did I imagine it? No, there he was waiting and gently whistling. What did happen next? I can't remember if I ran towards him—all I knew was that I wanted his arms around me and I was crying.

'Hey, hey,' He said 'What's the tears?' Told him what happened.

'I didn't expect to see you tonight. Didn't Shorty give you my message?'

'Sure but I thought I'd stick around anyway,' he grinned. Went out to our favourite garden seat—the night was warm. Jinx settled himself along the bench, his head in my lap. I liked that as I ran my fingers through his wavy hair. Felt like teasing him as I pulled a curl out, saying 'I love that tiny curl falling down your forehead—makes you look like Cupid!'

He frowned and I had great delight trying to smooth out the wrinkles on his brow.

'Stop frowning!' The man had gone to sleep! So much for his company, then remorse took over—he must be tired—let him sleep. And I realised that I like him—love—him. Could this be love that I've read and heard from others, if it is, I like it. I like the feeling of wanting to be close to someone I like—a good feeling, yes?

It was getting late. I had to wake him up.

'Have I been asleep?' What a silly question.

'My heavens!' he looked at his watch. 'Why did you let me sleep?' He was reproachful.

'You looked so tired and so comfortable I didn't have the heart to push you off the bench' I said. He stood up and I received my first kiss from Jinx. It—it was different—I don't think I saw any stars (according to the books) it felt like a touch of a butterfly it was that gentle and brief.

Walked back to the nurses' quarters where we said our goodnights—I had my second kiss—this time it wasn't so gentle nor was it as brief—in fact, I found it hard to breathe and had to push him so that I could get a gulp of air.

'Oh, Sheila!' he said, turned and quickly walked away.

Now, what did I do wrong? Have I offended him—will I see him again after this?

Friday, 12 October 1945

Five days—no Jinx! I have upset him—and I am missing him.

Lofty and Curly Top were having a discussion when I came off duty.

'Where's Glamour Boy?' asked Shorty when he saw me. 'Haven't seen him about lately.'

'Jinx a glamour boy?' I laughed. 'He is anything but . . .'

'Oh, all RAF chaps are glamour boys,' Shorty went on unperturbed by the laughter.

'After all, it isn't fair . . .'

'No, it isn't fair' echoed three of the convalescents.

'DO come out with us tonight. We've got a pass and besides tomorrow we'll be off' said the eldest one quietly.

Well, why not? Jinx hasn't been around and probably not likely to.

So off we went—the three 'Musketeers' as I called them. Jungle green uniforms and red berets—they did look smart and I was proud to be with them. Jack, the leader, hailed a taxi but I suggested walking was better for our health.

'Come on,' I said and slipping an arm through Jack's and Bill's I marched them along the road to the Great World.

'What would your wife say if she knew you are taking me out?' I asked Jack.

He grinned and said in the broad Yorkshire accent: 'Aw—she's a sensible wo-ooman, she is that.'

'And what about your girl, John?'

'Oh, she's probably doing the same thing—we fight and make up, fight and make up again.'

'And Bill—have you no one?'

'He's a lone wolf and beware of him, my girl,' I caught him wink at Bill.

I'm going to miss them . . .

As usual the Great World was crowded.

Sunday, 14 October 1945

Jinx was waiting for me. He had been ill—said MO wanted to send him here but said he wasn't that sick. Glad to see him and told him so.

'I've been worried' . . . 'Worried?' he said.

'You told me to stay away if I didn't feel well enough—really, you belong to a funny crew—you women!'

'I suppose we are' I admitted. Sat and talked about the future, talked around everything except what I really felt about him. What do you do—tell him I love him—ask him if he loves me? No, I couldn't do either of those things because I'm still not sure of this word 'Love' and what it means.

'By the way, Sheila, our squadron is giving a party next Friday at the Dutch Club. Some of the boys are going home—it's a sort of a send-off party. I'd like you to come and meet the boys.'

'I don't know, Jinx. Tomorrow I'll be leaving here with some of the other nurses. I'm being transferred to Kandang Kerbau Hospital and I hope to start my training there. And I won't know if I'll be off that night. Have to wait and see.'

Didn't make a late night tonight as I have an early shift in the morning.

Said goodnight at the front of the quarters—it seemed natural to kiss each other now—it makes me feel warm in his arms—only I wish he wouldn't hold me so tightly—it disturbs me. I feel nervous or something and yet I don't want him to let me go. Crazy woman that I am—I don't know what I want!

Friday, 19 October 1945

Excitement—day of the party. Had the evening off and a special pass from Matron. Some of the other nurses also invited. A gharry came to pick us up and transported us to the Dutch Club which was gaily lit—didn't take long for the dance floor to be crowded.

Jinx wasn't anywhere to be seen—my feelings of happiness vanished—he's not going to be here! Didn't have time to think when got whisked on to the dance floor. Asked my dancing partner if he knew Jinx—yes, he did and 'He's just coming in with a bunch of chaps'.

Suddenly I felt light-headed—wanted to rush to him but waited till the dance was over.

Jinx saw me and took me to his table. 'Come and meet the boys, Sheila—they are very, very anxious to meet you.'

So many of them—'This is Timmy our young artist; Willy, the best dancer in the squadron; Yorker our resident comic and of course, Brush, our CO' and there were more—how could I remember their names—told Jinx so.

'Never mind—as long as they know you. They'll never forgive me if I didn't introduce you. You see, they feel that they have a right to meet the girl who is taking so much of my thoughts and time.'

So-oo . . . He has been thinking of me—I wonder—and later I knew that he cared when he nearly had a fight with a sergeant who was dancing with me and who tried to kiss me. Seeing them measuring each other out in the garden, I couldn't help thinking that they were evenly matched and wondered that I could think of such a thing and quickly stood between them. It took a bit of persuading and Jinx let me lead him away from the sergeant.

'How dare he . . .'

'Don-t say it, Jinx—it's not worth it,' and I took his face in my hands and made him look at me. Next minute I was kissing him and I wanted him to keep on kissing me too—and this time I didn't mind him holding me tightly to him and I could feel his heart beating. I could have stayed like that all night I think, but it was him who pushed me away from him and said, 'I think it's time I took you home'.

Monday, 29 October 1945   Ward Two . . . 3 a.m.

On night duty past ten days—haven't been able to spend much time with Jinx but what time spent with him has been great.

Urgent message from Gauron to see him yesterday between 1–2 p.m. but overslept. However, went to Rex Hotel to inquire—met Lt Bradshaw—spoke to him and told to come and see him today at 4 p.m.—he said he had a reply from Australia and Auntie Grace can support me and willing to have me with her—will let me know as soon as arrangements can be made. Tonight when I see Jinx I will tell him—don't know if I want to go away now—I want to be with him—I love him, I do love him. Does he love me—he hasn't said so but then I haven't told him either.

Tuesday, 30 October 1945

Saw Jinx last night—told him that there is a chance that I may be going to Australia to live with my aunt. He was quiet for a moment, then 'That's good news, Sheila. I'm so glad for you—you'll have a better chance of doing something for your future.'

I'm afraid that wasn't exactly the reaction I wanted from him—wanted him to say he didn't want me to go and perhaps beg me to stay and be with him.

I stared at him, 'But I don't want to go—I want to be with you' I blurted out.

He put his arms around me and sighed. Instantly I sensed something wasn't right.

'What is it, Jinx? Have I said something, something I shouldn't?'

'Oh, Sheila, Sheila!' was all he said, then—'I'm not sure how you'll take this. Have been trying all week to tell you . . .' he stopped.

'Go on, Jinx. Something's happened—you don't want to see me any more. Is that it?' I felt my voice tremble.

'Have you been happy, Sheila?'

'Yes, oh yes when you are with me. It seems like a lovely dream but you do wake up from a dream, don't you?' I asked, somehow sensing that this dream of mine is going to be broken any minute.

'And to think that I'm the one to wake you up from this dream of yours. Doesn't seem fair, does it?'

'What do you mean?' and looked up at him. He was looking ahead with the frown that brought out the deep lines on his forehead.

'Dear Sheila, I wanted to tell you days ago but could not bring myself to say it. I too wanted this to last as long as it could but tonight I must . . .'

'You mean that—that you are leaving Singapore—when? Tomorrow?'

He could only nod his head.

Tomorrow, tomorrow he'll be gone—I had to think but how could I with his arms around me! Words tumbled as I told him of my feelings and desperately I clung to him, kissing him with utter abandonment. Then sanity prevailed as I realised the implication of our situation.

'Then this is goodbye?' I spoke into his jacket.

'Yes, Sheila. But you must go to your aunt and start a new life there—no, let me finish' as I tried to interrupt. 'Strange things happen sometimes and who knows our paths may cross again. Promise me that you'll go—one day you'll meet a man you'll love and marry and all this will be a memory and I hope, a happy one.'

How could he say that!

'I must go, Sheila—it's an early start for us tomorrow. And thank you, my Darling for just being you' and with a quick brush of his lips against mine he turned and walked away—away out of my heart—but he was whistling our tune, 'I'll Be Seeing You'. Yes! Jinx, I will be seeing you as the song says—'In all the familiar places Goodbye and Thanks for the memory'—I cried and how I cried!

Wednesday, 7 November 1945

Took myself off back to Sime Road Camp two days ago to see the 'girls'—had two days off and could not bear to be around the hospital after Jinx went. Oh, how I missed him and have kept myself busy to stop myself from thinking about him but the evenings—how lonely I felt!

It was good to see the girls—not many of them are there now—strange that I should want to go back there but it was the only 'bit' of home I had left and I knew I could be there on my own and 'lick my wounds' so to speak. I wandered around the camp and did a lot of thinking—such sad thoughts but there were also happy ones. I had time to review the past three and a half years as I turned the pages of my diary—I don't have to hide the books any more. Now I have all the time to write and record all that has happened since we were liberated without fear of being caught. Dear Diary—what would I have done without you.

Thursday, 8 November 1945   **Kandang Kerbau Hospital, Singapore**
12 noon—telephone call from Gauron in the Colonial Office—Flying tomorrow to Australia at 5.45 a.m.—to be ready—coming to see Matron about it afternoon.

2.30 p.m.—Gauron arrived—went to see Matron who was in a bad mood—said to see Col. Walkinshaw—up to him—wasn't very pleased about it but said we were also unprepared—anyway said wasn't going to stop me—to go and pack, etc. Asked Gauron if could fix me up either at Rex or Seaview for the night as difficult to get transport from Kandang Kerbau Hospital. Said see what could be done.

6 p.m.—Fixed up at the Rex—wrote letter to Matron thanking her. Had been invited to Paratroopers' Party at Blue Room—Pegasus Club—at first thought could not go but now decided to—so coming to Kandang Kerbau to be picked up later.

11.30 p.m.—Rex Hotel—had nice time—nearly danced off my feet—very friendly and when heard my last night in Malaya—would not let me sit down—saw Hastie—did not see me so tried to attract his attention—eventually succeeded—said for a moment could not recognise me. Came over and talked. Had a letter to me for 5 days—carried tonight with all the good intention of posting it—so gave to me when leaving. Also saw Lynamore and Douel—had one dance with the latter. The mental nurse was there—danced many times with him. Met several new chaps—extremely entertaining.

To be wakened at 4.30 a.m.—transport provided—to go with a Dr Goldberg.

Friday, 9 November 1945   10.30 a.m. on the plane (FD OV-VH-CTO)
Went in a saloon car driven by young RAPWJ chap—went to Kallang Airport—was raining! Hard too. Quite a number going. Had a cup of tea and sandwiches in the Buffet. Spoke to Lt Bradshaw—said goodbye to him—told me that everything will be fixed up in Australia. Hope so. Left Kallang Airport for Seletar Aerodrome—got onto this plane—21 passengers altogether with four others manning the plane—not very comfortable but can do. Left Singapore at about 5 a.m. The thrill of flying for the first time. Did not expect this—thought would go by ship in Feb but 'Teda ahpah' ['never mind'].

None of us was sick. Now flying over some islands—lovely to view country from above—everything looks like toys modelled in clay—think going to enjoy trip. Three children—a boy of 11 and two girls—one 6 and the other 5 years—very naughty—mostly Dutch and a few Australian soldiers—all to Australia . . .

Wednesday, 14 November 1945
1 p.m.—just left Townsville—had tiffin there at the Australian Red Cross—more

warmly welcomed than ever. Again names down—the place had flowers, fruit on tables and real food—it was heavenly! Arrived at about 11 a.m.—had left Port York at 6 a.m. after a good breakfast. Next stop Brisbane.

7.35 p.m.—Brisbane at last—arrived about 4 p.m. Had very rough flying— extremely cold—at one part was going to be sick and had a blackout but managed with an effort to pull myself up. The children and two other women were sick— worse off than myself.

Now put up at Red Cross Hostel, Story Bridge beside Waterloo Hotel—have our meals in the Hotel—two to a room. Warmly welcomed at the airfield. The Dutch had to go to the Dutch Camp and the British and Australian taken care of by the British-Australian Red Cross. At present in sitting room listening in to the radio. Discovered a fellow internee—a Mr Van Geyzel. Am with Miss Walshe (Irish) in room. Everyone is exceptionally kind. A girl in a green frock is coming in and talking to Mrs Williams and her son who were interned in Sumatra. She looks like a reporter and casting glances at me which means I'd better stop writing and probably have to answer some questions.

Thursday, 15 November 1945

1.45 p.m.—Had a very busy morning. A letter written to Jinx and went out with the Red Cross Sisters to be fitted out—took tram—got a few things and went to Allan and Stark to get a pair of shoes. Was a rush as had to be back at 1 p.m. for lunch otherwise get nothing. Had two pounds given and told if want some more to get in Sydney from Red Cross. People and traffic—can't get used to them. Saw many nice looking girls—some look like painted porcelain dolls, especially babies and children. Must get used to going about. Still plenty of servicemen about. The lady last night was a reporter all right.

The others talked a lot but I'm afraid I was yet too shy of speaking—wait till I get on my own, for as long as the others are willing to talk, I'll let them do so and reserve mine till a later date when probably the others are exhausted on the subject.

Rather warm in the house—outside sun shining brightly with a high wind blowing—nice weather. Have to sweep own room and keep place tidy.

9.20 p.m.—Had good afternoon sleep. After 7 p.m. went for a walk with Mrs Williams and son and Miss Walshe. Lovely nip in the air—went quite a long way off—saw amusement park and the Carnival for all servicemen. Had an ice-cream cone—and longing for Jinx—impossible to write anything more when in this mood. Have his picture before me and once again try to conjure his smile, hear his voice and feel his kisses and caresses—is this 'Love'? . . .

Saturday, 17 November 1945

Left Brisbane at 9 a.m. Stopped at Sydney for about 20 minutes. Arrive here about 3.30 p.m.—taken in the Red Cross car—lovely drive here—pretty place Melbourne. Auntie Grace—elderly and not unlike Dad in her ways. Warmly welcomed. Not her house—that was mortgaged when Grandad died but said had paid it all now and letting it to people—house called 'Hawthorn'. This house is 'Hartley'—nice one—a radio and a piano—3 bedrooms, bathroom, dining-sitting—breakfast room—kitchen etc. everything complete with a garden. Housekeeping for Mr T.H. White—an elderly gentleman, stout and white-haired. Feeling not quite at home yet—everything's so strange.

Sunday, 18 November 1945

Did not go out anywhere. Auntie had a lot to say about the family—only two of them but got a foster sister—'Olive' better known as 'Poppy'—about 25. Grandad died 9 years ago and Grandmother 17 years ago. Of Scottish-English descent— no Irish at all. Showed pictures—saw Dad when he was young—did not realise he was good looking as all that. There are lovely lots of books here. Played on the piano—didn't realise how stiff my fingers had gone. Wrote letters and am going to write some more. Had written to Jinx in Brisbane. Showed his photo to Auntie—thought he's a good-looking lad. Oh, I'm missing him more and more—I keep wanting him to be with me. I wonder if he's feeling the same or has he forgotten me and found someone more fascinating. Who knows—I may never see him again.

Tuesday, 20 November 1945

Went to the Red Cross House to get coupons—then to Mr Kirby about getting into Hospital said to try Nursing Association. Found that Dr Smallwood is here in South Yarra. Went to Pynes—bought a costume—black and braided—nice fit too—and some navy material for slacks. Two gardeners, spoke to them—nice gentlemen. Bought some stamps—the girl was very nasty. Went in a tram and came back in a train—first time in 4 years. Has been raining off and on. Never saw so many people in my life. The newspaper boys amuse me—also those people who look at me in their quizzical way. Our grocer is Chinese—had been in Singapore for three years—didn't like—said too hot all the time . . .

    Auntie: 'Do you like this boy very much?' looking at Jinx's photo. Nodded— 'I hope he's worthy of you'—

    'I think it's the other way round.'

    'Anyway, I hope he won't break your heart—men are so cruel, you know.'

Sighed, 'Yes, I know but my heart's not so easy to break now'. If it is Fate that we should not meet again—well, 'Tedah ahpah!' knowing full well that I'd feel dreadfully if that happens but then no one will know—it'll be my secret sorrow. Oh, God, I pray Thee to bring him back to me for I love him so but then if he doesn't love me?—well, in that case, it's my loss and nothing can be done about it.

Saturday, 24 November 1945

I have a very nice little room to myself and I do all my writing in here. Here I am—six stone 3 lbs! but Auntie Grace is feeding me so much that I feel more than that and to think I was nearly 10 stone before the war—what a fat pig I must have been!

Have to be at least 8 stone before I can start nursing—hopefully next year at the Queen Victoria Memorial Hospital.

Dear Diary, we have been on a long journey, you and I and now we have come to a crossroad. You and I must take our leave here—sadly I must say goodbye dear friend. Your journey is now ended and belongs to the past. Mine is the future—a road I must travel to begin a new life in Australia.

But you will not be forgotten, dear Diary. Your pages are my most precious memories of the past three and a half years of my life and I will remember again those experiences shared with my family and fellow internees. In time bitterness and sadness will be replaced by sympathy, understanding, and love towards others.

'Memories live longer than dreams

They are much stronger than dreams.'

So say words of a song. We've made our memories, you and I, Goodbye, dear, dear Diary but I will remember through your pages.

Postscript: 1992

Dear Diary, you and I are going on another trip—a trip down 'Memory Lane'—back to Singapore, Changi and Sime Road.

This time to find Dad's grave and to say farewell, not only to him but to those years spent in Camp—

Wednesday, 12 February 1992

Today I leave for Singapore with the RSL Travel group, organising the Reunion of the 50th Anniversary of the Fall of Singapore. It is a chance I am taking with the hope of finding Dad's grave while in Singapore.

Thursday, 13 February 1992

Arrived Singapore, Changi Airport 7.30 p.m. Staying at Miramar Hotel—room 602 on 6th Floor. There are 24 of us with June Healy as our Tour Leader.

Mary [Lim, née Winters, an ex-internee with whom I had kept in touch] had rung earlier so I returned her call at 11 p.m. and arranged to have lunch together tomorrow. It will be wonderful to see her again after all these years—what a lot of catching up to do and so little time to do it in!

Friday, 14 February 1992

Free morning—a chance to get to know my fellow travellers and what an interesting bunch they are—with stories to tell. How I wished I had brought my tape-recorder.

Had an enormous, absolutely delicious lunch! So much for all the warnings of not eating this and that! How I missed the Asian cuisine—nothing like the original!

3.15 p.m.—Attended the service at St Andrew's Cathedral—it was in this church that the injured were cared for during the bombing. I'm afraid I shed a few tears during the service.

5.45 p.m.—We were taken to the Australian High Commissioner Building for high tea (?) and welcoming speeches, etc. Being Chinese New Year—we were entertained by the 'Dragon Dancers'. Back at the hotel at 7.30 p.m. Had dinner and early to bed for an early start tomorrow.

Saturday, 15 February 1992
4 a.m.—Wake-up call. Quick breakfast and then taken to Krangi War Cemetery for the International POW Ceremony at 7.30 a.m. followed by plaque laying.

I can't describe this place—so big—so sad and yet so beautiful in its sadness. Everywhere I look I see rows and rows of headstones of those who have died in the Malayan Campaign. As I wandered along the rows of them—so young! What a waste of lives and yet not so—as they died so that we might live and we shall always remember them.

11 a.m.—Went into the city for the Civilian Service at the National Memorial (known as The Chopsticks).

12 noon—Met Fidelis and niece, Josephine, for an Indian lunch—a really 'hot' affair but I loved it!

Sunday, 16 February 1992
8.15 a.m. left the hotel for Krangi War Cemetery for a special 8th Division and War Widows' ceremony. It was a very moving service. We then did the north-west tour of the island where we looked out across the Straits of Johore to the mainland and I went back in memory as we crossed the causeway from Johore to escape the advancing Japanese and ended our journey in Singapore and internment!

Lunch in Changi Village and after lunch to Changi Prison for the unveiling of the plaque.

It has been a harrowing day in Changi Prison. All the way there I felt a strange uneasy feeling creeping over me. The road we drove over looked different and yet familiar in its direction. As we got further on I remarked to my fellow passenger that 50 years ago when I marched on this road with the others, there were only huts and kampongs along the way. I could almost feel the heat and dust and the flies as we trudged on. Malays lined the roadside to watch us.

As we neared the prison I started to breathe rather rapidly and desperately searched for my Ventolin puffer to ward off a wheezing attack. I ws still agitated when we went through those iron gates. The prison still looks the same inside—grey walls and cold! The guard who showed us around helped me to feel a little easier as we talked—he was interested in what I had to say about my stay here 50 years ago.

It was strange going up those iron stairs—those days the Japs' boots used to 'clang' up and down the stairs whenever they made their rounds of inspection and we would be fearful of the outcome of these visits.

Today as we walked up the steps—the sound is muffled. Looking into the cells, especially the ones I had occupied with two others, made me shudder a little as I thought of that cold hard cement slab under my body—the slab is no longer there today. The old style latrine is now replaced with a more modern cistern and there is a washbasin which we never had.

The hardest part was looking through the grille across the courtyard towards the Men's side. It was there that I would search for Dad's face behind the grille on his side. With our fingers through the grille we'd wave to each other to acknowledge our recognition.

Through misty eyes I took a long look at Changi Prison—I just don't want to see it again—I want to put it out of my life or can I? I don't know. I don't really know—part of my life is in these walls—can I really forget Changi Prison?

Went to the old Chapel and I am overwhelmed with sadness and on the spur of the moment I penned these words on the pages of a notebook—

Dad, I have not forgotten. Remembered with love. Sheila

John Charles Allan died 9th June 1945 in Sime Road Camp.

'Willie' [ABC TV cameraman] picked a single red hibiscus for me and I left it on the little altar with the other flowers there.

'Thank you, Willie' for your thoughtful gesture. Tomorrow I hope to be able to find Dad's grave.

10.30 p.m.—had a call from Mary—she has encountered some problems in locating the grave. As it was 47 years ago it means a manual search (no computers those days!) and that will take some time. She had explained that I will be leaving soon and needed to know before I left. Under the circumstances they are going to try their best for me.

Monday, 17 February 1992

Mary rang to say that the plot number is found and we are going to go to the cemetery at 9.30 a.m. and will pick me up at 9 a.m.

3 p.m.—Mary called to take me to have a look at the Sime Road, now called Adam Drive. The area now boasted some modern houses and driveways. It is a little hard to imagine the Camp as it was—no huts, no garden plots. The 'Dutch Club' as we used to call the meeting place is now a carport. The garden plots are overgrown with grass and weeds. There are big trees where huts used to be.

Looking around it I felt *nothing*—a blank as there is very little evidence to show what it was like then. Perhaps it's because we had more space to move around and being out in the open was a bonus after being cooped in Changi Prison.

There is nothing here to remind me of those days except for a patch of grassy plot where the nurses used to dance the Scottish dances on St Andrew's day. Nature has done her work well to cover up the area with trees and grass!

Tuesday, 18 February 1992

Today I found Dad's grave—how forlorn and uncared for in the midst of the others. There is nothing to mark his grave—no name, no number, nothing except perhaps a slightly raised mound.

Dad, I am sorry that I haven't come before this but I am here now and I will see to it that your final resting place is marked with your name—that is a promise I intend to keep. And I will be back to see that it is done. So many years and so many tears—once again I weep and wish you a final farewell—rest in peace now that I have at last found you and I will also find peace knowing that I have at last accomplished what I came to do.

Had our farewell dinner tonight. It has been an exhausting week, both physically and emotionally but I am glad I came. Have met and heard so many stories from the POWs—what a wonderful bunch of men—their experiences put mine in the shade! Yet, we were able to exchange stories and in many instances found that our stories were almost identical—to a lesser degree I went through some of what they had gone through. How did we ever manage to survive? But survive we did, and how!

Wednesday, 19 February 1992

We leave tonight for home. I look out of my hotel window and reflect on the scene below.

Singapore—how different it looks! Clean streets, trees lining the wide roads, buildings rising high towards the sky; people smiling; in their brightly coloured outfits, going about their affairs.

Fifty years ago, I see in my memory, a very different Singapore—a scene of devastation; buildings in ruins; dead and dying everywhere; the streets stained with blood! The Japanese bombs had done a lot of damage—acrid smoke-filled air and foul-smelling odour of rotting bodies would fill our lungs—a memory hard to erase!

As I look around, it looks as if the Almighty must have flung His arms over the city and let the floodgates open to sweep away all that remained of war-torn Singapore and out of the ruins rose the tall buildings that now outline the sky.

The Singapore of today is not the Singapore of my yesteryears. Today is the Present—Yesterday with its memories is the Past and I only know that Past.

And so, my Dear Diary, I will finally say goodbye to that Past—not forgetting what is Past but to go on living and praying that the Past will not happen again.

So ends my story . . . Wednesday 19th February, 1992 . . . Singapore. And I quote:

> And we that are left
> Grow old with the years
> Remembering the heartache
> The pain and the tears;
> Hoping and praying
> That never again man will sink
> To such sorrow and shame.
> The price that was paid
> We will always remember
> Every day, every month
> Not just in November.

End of quote.